WHEN WILL THE LIGHTS GO OUT?

D0928747

WHEN WILL THE LIGHTS GO OUT?

Derek G Birkett

STACEY
INTERNATIONAL

When Will the Lights Go Out?

STACEY INTERNATIONAL

128 Kensington Church Street

London W8 4BH

Tel: +44 (0)20 7221 7166; Fax: +44 (0)20 7792 9288

Email: info@stacey-international.co.uk

www.stacey-international.co.uk

ISBN: 9781906768409

CIP Data: A catalogue record for this book is available from the British Library

1 3 5 7 9 0 8 6 4 2

Printed in Turkey by Mega Basim

CONTENTS

Foreword

This is a staggering book, warning the country that our electricity supplies are in danger. It should perhaps have a different title to *When Will the Lights Go Out?* and be called instead, *The Lights Will Go Out.*

Mr Birkett has been responsible for the operation of the National Grid in the Highlands of Scotland and elsewhere in the UK. In that capacity he has been responsible for the two most important forms of new energy – hydro-electricity and nuclear electricity. He has also had considerable experience with gas and renewables.

Our problem is that in the 2010s, North Sea oil will be a declining contributor. Our old gas plants will probably have break-downs. The Blair-Brown Government announced the phasing out of some of our older nuclear power stations and the supply of gas is affected by a lack of storage space. All of these combine to make soaring electricity prices a feature of the next few years, along with power cuts due to break-downs and sheer unavailability.

Part of the danger is caused by the Government's decision to focus on global warming, doubtless knowing this would be understandably popular with the electorate in the run-up to the 2010 General Election. Without Proper consideration they announced a target of 20 per cent of our energy to come from renewable sources by 2020. Their main solution was wind power, which everyone knows is massively expensive and massively unreliable. When the wind stops the energy stops and you have to have a standby power station providing electricity when this happens. When the wind is too high the system has to be stopped because of the potential damage to the wind installations.

In California, with ideal prevailing winds throughout the year, a Governor of the State who was attracted by the appeal to the electors of renewable energy heavily subsidised wind power companies. Most of these companies are now in Chapter 11 having their bankruptcy attended to while receiving even greater subsidies. In this country I know of no investor who would invest in windmills unless they were heavily subsidised by the Government, which they are. Meanwhile, this target will not be achieved. What it has done is to put at disadvantage other sound forms of new energy supply such as hydro-electricity and nuclear electricity.

If there was a National Syllabus I would make this book part of it and I would see that it had to be read by Members of Parliament, the Cabinet and the Shadow Cabinet. There should be an annual budget for electricity setting out the targets to avoid the lights going out. Lights going out due to lack of electricity closes factories, closes schools and creates unemployment – in fact it is a disaster. Governments should be seen budgeting to take action to minimize the loss of electricity in this country.

Lord Walker of Worcester MBE PC,
May 2010

Author's Preface

When compiling this book I have been aware that without the support and encouragement of others it could never have been written. These friends and colleagues have been brought together by a common understanding and experience of times when generation supply dominated the economic activity of this nation. To satisfy rising demand for electricity arising from improving living standards, immense resources of capital, manufacture and skill were required. This was a period when many of my working colleagues had experienced the rigours of wartime adversity, rubbing off onto me attitudes of frugality, humour and not least an awareness of giving something back for the sacrifices made by others.

The long period of peace and prosperity enjoyed by our nation has eroded these qualities to be replaced by concern for personal gain and a decline in public standards and confidence in our institutions. The inability of most citizens to consider the longer term is reflected in the dire circumstance the nation now finds itself. This book attempts to explain a looming crisis in one of the least discussed aspects of our problem, that of energy security and electricity supply. Preoccupation with global warming has concealed a neglect for a balanced strategy of generation provision, a requirement not understood by the public at large who simply take for granted electricity will always be there at the flick of a switch. The gravity of this position has yet to penetrate the public mind but its ramifications are every bit as serious as the financial crisis recently experienced. If this book can provide some understanding to the reader of the issues involved it will have served its purpose.

In many ways the book follows on from the inspiration given by Dr John Etherington's excellent book *The Wind Farm Scam* published by Stacey International exposing the ill-thought-out policy of wind resource for electricity generation. We had previously been in email contact and the discussions held were a source of information to both of us. Another mutual colleague and friend, Dr Alan Shaw has provided a most readable historical account of electricity supply and this is contained as the first appendix within this book. I would thank him most warmly for his contribution. I am most grateful to Lord Walker for his encouraging remarks in the Foreword and prescient comment. We share the need for public awareness of the critical issues facing electrical supply in the years ahead. Essential logistical support has been supplied by David Bruce over many years, and his analysis of the narrative was instrumental in having the book accepted for publication. Neil McKinnon and Angela Kelly have both provided unstinting source material over the years which is reflected in the references at the end of each chapter. Numerous other individuals, too many to name have contributed in so many different ways and their support has been valued if remaining unacknowledged. Above all it has been the encouragement of Ron and Helen Quartermaine over most of this decade where the necessary inspiration and advice originated, creating the conditions for setting out on this project. Their hospitality, support and guidance have been the foundation upon which all the aforementioned have contributed. To all these people I extend my gratitude and appreciation for their unwavering support, without which this book could never have been written. It is in large measure their achievement, although the responsibility for what has been written is mine alone.

Derek G Birkett,
May 2010

Introduction

A Journey to see the Emperor's New Clothes

To sustain interest in this book much of the essential technical content has been contained within the notes and appendixes. Repetition is used to emphasise critical issues. Throughout, a conscious effort has been made to limit numerical technical detail, in particular with costs that rapidly become dated. The devil is in the detail and the facts revealed hold profound economic and political consequences. The message is a simple one: the fixation on renewable energy as is being developed will just not work on the scale being promoted. Current policies will make electricity costs damaging to industry and increase fuel poverty.

Experience gained by the author over twenty years as a grid control engineer in north Scotland has been supplemented by direct operational contact with coal and hydro generation. Over a decade was spent on project installation and commissioning at five power station locations, three of which were nuclear, with the old Central Electricity Generating Board (CEGB) and The Nuclear Power Group (TNPG) nuclear consortia organisations. This experience gave the award of chartered engineer, following graduation as an electrical engineer. Knowledge gained has been based upon hands-on experience yet information was always to hand. However knowledge and experience are one thing, putting one's head above the parapet is another. Being retired greatly eases this difficulty.

This journey began when a specific proposal for an extensive wind farm was proposed just four miles from my home, located in one of the most scenic parts of Highland Perthshire. Consultations with local councils revealed the inadequacy of knowledge and absence of central directing principles. The Scottish Executive attempts to support a renewable agenda through initial discussions and sponsored academic papers confirmed that the intent to fully develop wind resource was real and substantial. This myopic scenario was anathema to my whole working experience and that of many of my professional colleagues, being driven by a combination of political ineptitude and commercial opportunity. As an enthusiastic hill-walker and single-handed sailor off the Scottish west coast, the vagaries surrounding wind behaviour were well known.

Sailing provides a sound analogy for grid operation. The vessel has to be adequate for the sea conditions and good judgement exercised to reach the required destination. The most direct course is not always the most secure. Many hazards need to be avoided and the unexpected overcome. It is the juxtaposition with more than one of the many unanticipated variables where failure arises. Problems come in threes it is said and while provision is invariably made to accommodate any single item, when combined together they become sufficient to overwhelm the resources available. A study of the grid incidents later mentioned reveal just how true is this observation.

History gives many examples where institutional direction of technology has been confounded by experience. Decisions that initially seemed logical and desirable rapidly changed with events. The provision of electrical energy is no exception; strategic political direction through subsidy has created an extensive commercial interest based upon renewable resources, primarily wind. This technology is impressive but its useful application is confounded by the intermittence of its availability. Expertise is limited to a few score of individuals able to operate the Electricity Grid systems where such power has to be accommodated. Such systems vary in scale and nature where control problems arising all require an independent solution by experienced personnel. To communicate this problem is not straightforward and best illustrated by analogy.

When stacking jam jars a surprising number can be removed without collapsing the structure. This depleted structure can stand for long periods but inevitably external vibration will introduce collapse. Such is the nature of the problem when introducing uncontrollable generation onto a delicately balanced grid system, regardless of the ingenuity employed with offsetting measures.

By good fortune, becoming associated with a group of like-minded professionals from varied backgrounds with high technical responsibility, it became clearer to see the devastating consequences that would follow such misguided direction. This was not just an ascetic revulsion with landscape desecration but a disastrous direction of energy policy, already fatally weakened by the flawed decision to dismantle the old CEGB organisation. In my becoming honorary secretary of this informal technical group, information was circulated across all aspects of energy development, the use of the internet and email communication becoming an indispensable tool.

Prior to this opportunity participation at three public inquiries was made, two for wind farm applications and the third for the Beauly-Denny 400kV transmission line application. This latter project, spread across some of the most sensitive Highland landscape in Scotland, was not without alternative solutions. This experience revealed the flawed prospectus driving the project forward with inadequate structural and technical safeguards in place preventing a more informed outcome.

Increasing concern and information gave me encouragement to participate in various consultation exercises initiated by the Royal Society of Edinburgh, the House of Lords, Department of Business, Enterprise and Regulatory Reform and the National Grid. Although the latter two were seen as being largely cosmetic, an opportunity was given to record some statement. Critically the control position of National Grid was perceived as becoming increasingly untenable following the grid incident of 27 May 2008. By coincidence, a visit to their national control room had been arranged for the following week, together with a party of senior engineers from the nuclear industry. The subsequent delayed reports from this grid incident gave no convincing cause to explain the extensive loss of supply; my background as a grid system control engineer had made me conversant with system fault reporting.

It was only during 2009 that the concern over generating capacity provision on the GB system became a public issue, a condition well known for years by many with technical understanding of the electricity supply industry. The fact that politicians have put the nation into this predicament can be explained, though not excused, by the remarkable lack of technical guidance emanating from their civil servants. Essentially this is a cultural problem permeating most of current British society. The huge scale of resources required to overcome this crisis has yet to be addressed, diverted by self-inflicted environmental and political constraints, creating extensive uncertainty into areas of investment with real need. To cut the knot, the one message that should emerge from this impending catastrophe can be summed up in two words, 'forget renewables'.

To many this will sound like heresy in the climate of thought existing over dubious global warming concerns. The response is one of perspective, knowledge and realism where on this journey the reasons for this conclusion will be explained with an instinct for practical workable solutions. In so many ways we are victims of the global circumstance in which we live, in this over-populated world of today, so very different from the frugal upbringing of our fathers in what used to be the cradle of industrial power that has so transformed our modern world.

Terminology

The basic unit of power is the watt. In terms of domestic consumption the old incandescent light bulb would typically have a rating of 60 Watts (W) or 100W whereas a single bar on an electric fire would usually rate at 1,000W or 1 kilowatt (1,000 watts) (kW). Using this single bar for an hour would consume one unit or 1 kilowatt-hour (kWh) of electricity. When multiplied by one thousand it becomes 1 megawatt-hour (MWh). MW represents a measure of energy capacity, MWh represents the time that this capacity is exercised to give a quantity of energy. For most applications these terms should be sufficient but can be extended as follows:

- A generator of 1kW installed capacity if run for one hour would produce 1kWh of energy (a unit).
- A generator of 1kW run for a year continuously would produce 8760kWh (units) or 8.76MWh.
- A generator of 1MW run for a year continuously would produce 8.76GWh or 8.76 million units.
- One thousand generators of 1MW, or 1GW (gigawatt), run for one year produce 8.76TWh.

On occasion, a measure of capacity (MW) may be represented by mega volt ampere (MVA) as with transmission lines and transformers. In power terms they mean the same but allow for a reactive component (capacitive or inductive) which increases the current rating.

1 The UK Structure for Electrical Supply

Be sure your sin will find you out.

Book of Numbers

Looking to the future it is always wise to study the past. An absorbing submission from Dr Alan Shaw to the Royal Society of Edinburgh (RSE) in 2006 gives an historical summary of the development of Electrical Supply in the UK (*Appendix 1*). This paper should give a necessary grounding into the complexity of electrical supply and is suggested reading.

There are two essential facts to understand about electrical power. It cannot be stored on any appreciable scale and it cannot be spilled. As a consequence power must be produced as required instantaneously; any deviation affects system frequency, reducing induction motor performance for auxiliaries that sustain generation output. To protect the whole grid system from instability and collapse, automatic disconnection of consumers is triggered outside certain limits. It needs little imagination to become aware of the extensive consequences that follow any disconnection of power in our complex technology-based society. Any extended loss of electrical power would be likely to result in civil disorder in most of our major cities. This circumstance should be seriously considered when making decisions to impose unprecedented, extensive, intermittent and uncontrollable forms of generation supply onto this unforgiving beast of a grid system. Until now this nation has been spared excessive disruption but events overseas, and periodic close calls in this country, remind grid controllers of an intrinsic vulnerability within grid networks.

Electrical power today is distributed by fourteen regional suppliers from a single centrally operated high voltage (HV) national grid that covers Great Britain's mainland, known as the GB Grid system. In Scotland the grid transmission system is owned by the constituent power companies. Most generating capacity is fed into this high voltage system from power stations with a range of fuel technologies having varying constraints of start-up notice, loading versatility and maintenance requirements. Existing interconnections from other grid systems are made with Northern Ireland and France through high voltage direct current (HVDC) sub-sea cabling, additional connections being under discussion.

Generation of power into this GB Grid system has to satisfy an annual demand approaching 400 terawatt-hours (TWh) where the baseload component provides 55% of annual energy production. The minimum generation capacity that is required over the summer period is 40% of the winter peak requirement at around 60GW. However with increasing levels of 'embedded' generation derived from combined heat and power (CHP) schemes, wind and other renewable sources produced within the distribution networks, these parameters are set to change quite significantly. Such uncontrolled sources from a grid perspective are seen as 'negative demand' to the GB Grid system.

The benefit of having alternating current (AC) supply is its versatility in transforming voltages to reduce power losses in conductors across the network. It is only with continental distances that the use of direct current (DC) becomes an economic proposition for transmitting power with overhead lines. For sub-sea connection where cabling becomes necessary, technical limitations oblige AC power transfers to be restricted by distance. HVDC provides a means of connecting independent high voltage alternating current (HVAC) grid systems to enable power exchanges, without compromising the operational integrity of the respective systems.

Before privatisation was introduced in 1990 the old Central Electricity Generating Board (CEGB) organisation had responsibility for both transmission and generation with centralised strategic forward planning. The changes brought about dismembered this structure, placing reliance on market mechanisms to provide generation scheduling and future investment. The role of National Grid became confined to ownership of transmission assets in England and Wales and the crucial function of system balancing as Transmission System Operator (TSO). Large-scale generation is confined to half a dozen main players, broadly shared between nuclear, coal and gas fuel sources. Some oil capacity exists but has rare use, soon to be retired under the EU Large Combustion Plant Directive (LCPD) together with a substantial coal component. There is no overseeing technical authority to determine strategic forward planning although monitoring is undertaken by transmission owners with their Seven Year Statements (SYS). The dominant position of National Grid enables technical standards embodied in the Grid Codes to be implemented under the umbrella of GB Security and Quality of Supply Standards (GB SQSS) requirements.

Within generation capabilities from each fuel source there are wide variations of response. These are outlined in *Appendix 2* and have critical importance for meeting the instantaneous balancing requirement to maintain an operating system frequency between statutory limits[1]. This is a crucial function to ensure system stability. In a wider sense all fuel sources have a complementary function with one another and are mutually supporting to give the most overall economic level of generation capability. Known as the generation mix, in sum total it has to exceed the winter maximum demand by a substantial margin, usually set at 20% to allow for breakdown of plant, abnormal demand and errors in estimation. In the absence of forward planning since privatisation, no single body carries overall responsibility and with inadequate government energy policy, a situation has developed where this generation mix has become seriously distorted. It will take decades to restore a proper balance.

Stability of the GB Grid system is not confined to essential balancing of load with generation supply but extends to maintaining a stable voltage (pressure) profile over the transmission network to ensure that predictable power flows are maintained[2]. These frequent adjustments from a range of voltage modifying equipment can be as necessary to stability as the more obvious need to balance supply and demand. This is why the GB Grid system can be described as a dynamic, unforgiving beast, inherently unstable. The introduction of widespread renewable generation sources without constraint creates a situation where controllable generation has to 'dance around' or accommodate these wayward members, in addition to normal consumer demand variations. To a considerable extent demand is predictable, intermittent wind is not, and reliance on dispersion only increases the scale of potential variation.

Transmission

The role of transmission in developing new generation has been little understood outside discrete technical circles. Yet its environmental impact is every bit as significant as the furore over wind farm construction. This reflects not only the need to connect the numerous dispersed site locations but the necessity of trunk reinforcement with existing infrastructure. The cost of this connection and support is aggravated by the low utilisation attending renewable generation, especially with that from wind resource. In addition because of its size, the introduction of continental nuclear technology presents major reassessments for the GB Grid system to cope with a single event loss[3].

A notable characteristic of the GB Grid system is its elongation and proximity to Atlantic weather systems. It is between a sixth and seventh of the size of the continental grid system, which has the advantage of scale to give stability and a secure French nuclear base load at the centre of a large interconnected system. Most nations within this network also have a substantial hydro component providing fast response support for peak demands as well as for wind intermittence.

The GB Grid system operates at the high voltage levels of 400 kilovolts (kV) and 275kV except for Scotland where with so many generation in-feeds, mainly of hydro, a lower grid voltage of 132kV has been maintained. Consequently, many onshore wind farms in Scotland are monitored whereas in England and Wales only offshore schemes become eligible. There is another characteristic with the Scottish network of far reaching significance. The transmission system is not strongly connected to England, extending throughout the northern region. Power flows steadily increase as passage is made towards the southeast. Transmission charges to users therefore reflect an incentive to connect generation in the south of the GB Grid system rather than the north where most renewable potential is available.

Government policy to meet renewable targets, supported by the political agenda of a devolved Holyrood administration, has encouraged extensive short time-scale development of wind resource on a scale that introduces a number of transmission constraints. These have the potential for severe cost penalties that ultimately fall upon the electricity consumer. The industry regulator Ofgem has estimated these costs to be £262 million for 2009/10[4]. These relate to:

Cross Border Interconnection

There are two major transmission lines that need to be upgraded, necessitating summer outages that will limit the export capability from Scotland during that period. With low summer demand, nuclear baseload generation and other committed generation, the freeboard for intermittent wind production is not high and would introduce constrained off procedures where generous compensation is given for the generators affected. Even on completion of this interconnection upgrade, the rapidly increasing capacity of wind resource will re-address this constraint introducing further compensation payments to generators.

Approval for Premature Connection

To enhance capacity targets, approval in principle has been given by the government for transmission connection to be brought forward for schemes that otherwise would have to await reinforcement of the grid infrastructure. This decision introduces an operational dimension that inevitably will initiate constrained off procedures and subsequent costs on a regular basis. The scale of this approval is almost half that of existing hydro capacity within the Highlands[5].

Maintenance and Project Requirements

The siting of most wind farm schemes has largely been determined by existing transmission infrastructure, bringing the network to its full capability in many places. Throughout an extended summer season, maintenance demands of not just the lines themselves but related substation equipment dictate outages, restricting the operating capability of the network and consequential constrained off payments. With so much project activity on upgrading, replacement and enhanced capability for substation equipment, these outage demands are considerably extended and can be inflated with proximity outages from adjacent circuits.

Recent proposals to strengthen the border interconnection have moved away from a third transmission line towards HVDC undersea cable links along both west and east coasts with likely destinations in proximity to the Dee and Tyne estuaries[6]. Inevitably, these projects would become embroiled with connections for offshore wind development and the proposal for an offshore super-grid. There is an increasing tendency to promote continental interconnection as an antidote to overcome intermittence arising from the renewable commitment by government policy[7] (*Appendix 5A*). This circumstance could easily drift into a situation of reliance where the GB Grid system would have a one-way dependency upon the continental grid and vulnerability to offshore terrorism. HVDC cable can have high reliability but the incidence of fault involves extended periods for repair, certainly for winter marine conditions. Overhead transmission has more fault exposure to the elements but access allows much faster restoration times.

Loss of supply to customers are averaging at less than 100 minutes each year while grid transmission failure amounts to only 1% of this average. However a single major grid incident as experienced in May 2008 could easily cause an equivalent of ten to twenty years of 'normal' unavailability in one day[8]. Network conductor losses in distribution supply are around four times the level met with on the main transmission grid.

Organisational Structures

If past success is any guide for the future then experience from nationalisation should be heeded. An organisation was created, led and managed by technical expertise and made publicly accountable for the supply and distribution of electricity supply throughout the UK. The explosion of electricity demand in the 1960s would double over seven years. This technical and constructional challenge was successfully met by structures with long-term planning, effective regulation and a dedicated workforce having a sense of public ethos. Its failures were political in origin with subservience to the Treasury, premature construction of power stations and neglect to open coal to competitive tender. It also became increasingly bureaucratic. Crucially, except for Scotland where supply was vertically integrated, transmission and generation were combined into one structure known as the Central Electricity Generating Board (CEGB). Although a monopoly, this body had sufficient industry knowledge and institutional weight to overcome many political vicissitudes, providing continuity and long term vision. For many years, it resisted the large-scale adoption of gas turbine technology as a strategic choice. Many changes followed from privatisation where market forces were allowed free reign. One predictable consequence has been the termination of new nuclear build, another the abdication of responsibility where no one body was in overall charge. Centralised long term planning and research were discontinued. Much information became inaccessible with commercial confidentiality. For twenty years, the only new significant generation source for grid connection was with gas turbine technology. The scheduling of generation plant, previously done on a merit order principle, is now conducted on a contract basis, experiencing three upheavals of procedure within four years, leading directly to the near bankruptcy of British Energy[9]. For over a decade the only Government policy was for renewable development, with the incumbent Minister being changed on an annual basis, not even having cabinet rank. Only as late as 2008 was nuclear generation reluctantly promoted. Recent political restructuring has combined energy and climate change, both functions being mutually incompatible, only addressing the yawning gap over generation capacity this coming decade by continued gas installation.

Summary

The GB Grid system is inherently unstable and must constantly balance supply and demand from a range of generation technologies. Major changes followed privatisation in 1990. Transmission infrastructure is a key consideration when developing renewable resource, with major constraints across the Scottish border interconnection. Recent developments promote further interconnection in conjunction with offshore wind resource exploitation.

Notes and References
1. Normal operating frequency fluctuates between 49.8Hz and 50.2Hz. Statutory limits are at 49.5Hz and 50.5Hz.
2. Operational standards ensure the loss of any transformer, generator or double circuit transmission line will not result in an unacceptable operating condition.
3. The maximum single event loss is currently 1320MW based upon reactor loss at Sizewell B. The new continental reactor designs are expected to raise this threshold towards 1800MW.

4. Ofgem letter 17/2/2009 – *Managing constraints on GB Transmission System*.

5. Ofgem press release R/21 of 8/5/2009 – *Connection of 450MW low carbon generation*.

6. DECC ENSG Report 4/3/2009 p65 fig 5.4 – *Our Electricity Network: A Vision for 2020* http://www.ensg.gov.uk/assets/ensg_ transmission_ pwg_full_report_final_issue_1.pdf

7. DECC ENSG Report 4/3/2009 p38 fig 2.5 – *Our Electricity Network: A Vision for 2020*.

8. *Power Engineering Journal* – October 2002 p241 – *Power System Security*.

9. A system of contract scheduling for generation was set up at privatisation known as the Pool. About the millennium this was changed to a new system known as NETA becoming BETTA.

2 Generation Technologies

Electricity is the life blood of the nation – without it we perish.

At some stage in the operational life of all generation technologies each source has to be seen to be economic. Investment has to consider a typical thirty-year duration for thermal plant where capital costs vary, running costs fluctuate and technical advances change considerably over this period. Capital pay-back periods are a critical parameter where operational life can range from twenty years for a wind turbine to almost a century with hydroelectric resource where capital expenditure is largely spent on civil engineering works.

To use a military comparison, a battalion in barracks needs never fire a shot in anger to be effective, their very presence can suppress disorder. In such a strategic industry as power generation this analogy applies to fuel sources for generation supply where concentration on one source becomes an economic Achilles heel. This is what maintaining a generation mix means and why it is so essential. This chapter explains the main characteristics behind each generation technology.

Nuclear Generation

For baseload operation, nuclear generation is the most advantageous form of generation, but it requires high capital investment and long construction timetables. Secure fuel sources and a limited fuel cost component ensure a stable and reasonably predictable generation cost. However, when Sizewell B in Suffolk was commissioned in the early nineties, the intended successor power stations did not materialise. The episode when British Energy almost became bankrupt, caused by the financial goalposts being moved and culminating with the sale of Westinghouse (a nuclear design company) to foreign interests, prevented any prospect of indigenous new construction. Only in 2008 did government give recognition for a nuclear programme that with necessary regulation and license approval implies a minimum ten-year period before power becomes available. In a global market with escalating interest in a nuclear option in the developed world, critical manufacturing constraints and credit concerns could well extend this time estimate.

The remaining nuclear capacity of AGR design is rapidly ageing. To extend operational life certain stations have loading restricted to 70% of nominal capacity. Most capacity is expected to retire over the coming decade although official optimism with plant extension would extend the dates as given with the British Energy sale prospectus of November 2008. New capacity of continental design, presently under assessment, will significantly raise the threshold of any single event loss upon the grid network. This consequence would require a higher operational standby contingency as well as extensive design re-assessment within the existing transmission network. The cost implications will be severe. The whole programme should have commenced a decade earlier, as was the original intention, with an indigenous design.

Aversion to nuclear power has concentrated on the hazard with nuclear waste material. What is not widely known is that technical means to overcome this hazard have been in place for over thirty years. The reluctance of politicians to legislate has created a dispersal of built up waste at each power station location, instead of at a single secure underground depository. The waste quantities involved are manageable, where any new supply would be dwarfed by existing material in cooling ponds. This stockpile represents a significant energy resource if re-circulated through the medium of fast breeder technology; an option discontinued through nuclear proliferation concerns.

Coal-fired Generation

The position of coal is also insecure and uncertain. This arises from an age profile when most capacity was constructed over the late sixties and seventies, the last major station being at Drax, Yorkshire in the mid 1980s. Two significant obstacles are present because of environmental regulation that introduces constraints. The first is the European Union Large Combustion Plant Directive (EU LCPD) by which costly flue cleaning equipment must be fitted by the middle of the coming decade to comply with rigorous emission standards. Given the age of existing plant this expense in many instances is not warranted. Significant capacity will become retired for this deadline, if not earlier with the restriction of permitted running hours before this deadline is reached. This constraint extends beyond 2016 by a replacement regulatory instrument known as the Industrial Emissions Directive (IED) extending until 2023 with tightening annual emission limits and restricted running hours[1].

The second obstacle is the expectation for new investment to be fitted with Carbon Capture and Storage (CCS) equipment, an unproven technology with high operational cost. Furthermore uncertainty arises with recent calls for new gas turbine power stations to be fitted with this CCS technology, though emissions are about half that for coal[2].

Coal generation is far more suited for load following, a facility that would become much more necessary with increasing renewable development. The supply of indigenous coal has shrunk in recent years with overseas competition but coal remains a necessary bulwark against the dominance of gas supplies. Generating capacity constraints in the UK over this coming decade raises the question of relaxing the LCPD directive, a defining moment for political direction. There are also two technical developments that influence future investment in coal capacity. Superheated technology enables far higher fuel efficiencies to be realised than currently exists in the UK. Another development is in experimental clean coal technology where fuel combustion can be accommodated within gas turbines, avoiding the closed steam/feed-water cycle thereby reducing capital costs[3].

Hydroelectric Generation

The availability, durability and loading versatility with this technology is superior to any other form of generation. This has been exploited to provide the only effective means of storing energy by the technique of pumped storage. However a number of constraints exist to limit future deployment. Overall efficiency is around two-thirds after hydraulic and conductor frictional losses. Sites are restricted to mountainous regions that require a lower large volume freshwater reservoir, adjacent to an upper high head storage reservoir of sufficient capacity to absorb a full day of generation. Such sites are rare and need to be sited to limit transmission losses. Constructional costs are high and site sensitive where dam and tunnel expense predominates. Existing plant is located in the Scottish Highlands and North Wales, where most capacity is located in Snowdonia although here the upper storage capacity is limited.

The unsung success story of UK power supply must rest with conventional hydroelectric generation largely located in the Scottish Highlands. Most capacity was developed in the post-war years until the early sixties and has reliably and consistently provided a sizeable proportion of Scottish electricity demand, currently a tenth. It is surprising with current enthusiasm for renewable sources, that more attention has not been focussed on this technology as available potential could replicate existing development. Certainly the Glendoe scheme, the first of any size for fifty years, and a number of small schemes have recently been constructed but much remains. This could be for a combination of reasons but primarily capital return where long-term development is not encouraged in a climate of quick fix, variable subsidy solutions as with wind technology. The concern of piecemeal private development trammelling the larger storage schemes is a risk where any comprehensive development requires the commitment of large corporations with longer-term perspective[4].

Statistical information reveals a misleading low availability. This is a reflection of designed load factor avoiding unnecessary spillage and is site specific. The nature of this resource with its operational flexibility makes it ideally suited for fast response reserve at premium prices. This would correspond with the increasing fluctuation of intermittence inherent with other renewable resource. Even if fully developed, the contribution of hydroelectricity towards meeting our power needs is marginal at best, unlike our continental neighbours where existing capacity has a prominent role in overcoming intermittence with their own wind portfolios.

Gas Turbines

Apart from the nuclear power station at Sizewell whose inception predated privatisation, all grid connected conventional generating capacity since 1990 has been of gas turbines. This takes two forms, open circuit and closed circuit. The former provides quick start-up plant for use as emergency response. The second category of closed circuit gas turbines (CCGT) utilise gas fuel much more efficiently by recycling exhaust heat but with the disadvantage of restricting their operating range and response capability. Most capacity is of the closed circuit form with relatively short construction time-scales and lower capital cost than alternative fuel sources. Generation charges are much more sensitive to fluctuations with the cost of gas supplies, introducing price and supply volatility.

There are other concerns with gas turbine generation. Frequent load cycling increases maintenance demands and reduces availability. Type faults could arise where metal temperatures operate at the limits of designed capability. Probably the greatest concerns are strategic with fast depleting reserves of North Sea gas and insufficient national storage capacity available. Alternative gas sources from overseas are less secure than other fuel sources. With any restriction of supply, the domestic market would take prior call over power generation, given the safety issues arising from disconnection. The only effective antidote in this situation would be price inflation and a commercial means of reducing price volatility. The main concern with the use of gas for electricity generation is its efficiency of utilisation. Only about half of the heat content is converted to electrical energy when compared to heating supplies for domestic or industrial use. While at first glance this point seems academic, its ramifications extend into the strategic arena with implications for being sustained over the longer term.

Renewable Resource

Increasing environmental and political pressure has promoted a range of uneconomic renewable technologies by subsidy, financed through opaque mechanisms initiated by government and ultimately funded by the electricity consumer. Initially this subsidy supported landfill gas extraction but increasing wind resource has now become the dominant technology. Normally subsidy can be justified to kick start a developing technology into commercial viability but this consideration has long since been discounted for wind resource. The intended scale of wind technology being promoted by government policy has highly significant and adverse consequences.

A major problem of wind resource is not just intermittence alone but with its prediction. A study of the output characteristics for a 2.5 megawatts (MW) wind turbine indicates 70% of its upper range of output is confined to only two categories on the Beaufort Wind Scale, that of fresh and strong breeze. With excessive wind speeds turbines shut down automatically. To mitigate these constraints, reliance is placed upon diversity, a dubious solution only serving to reduce the incidence of overall intermittence, not eliminate it, incorporating less productive capacity.

The energy contribution from wind has now overtaken conventional hydroelectric generation. Because intermittence is seen as 'embedded generation' and as 'negative demand' other controllable generation has to accommodate its varying output as a standby facility. The range and duration of this support fluctuates widely, introducing substantial operational cost penalties. Initial forecasts of load factor for wind resource over the UK have been found to be grossly optimistic, limiting energy output, raising capacity requirements to meet renewable targets and diminishing its contribution for firm supply. This last item has significant consequence in reducing any statistical contribution towards peak demands on the system, which must be found from other generation sources. This has led to a situation where almost all wind capacity needs replication by conventional means.

This critical fact leads on to the problem of having to finance standby capacity. On plant other than base-load, an assessment has to be made of projected load factor for any investment over its operational life. With significant renewable generation the scope for available running is reduced thereby compromising the viability of the standby investment. Inevitably this would introduce further subsidy above the enormous intended scale of wind resource capacity implicit with government renewable targets. This absurd situation has recently been exposed in a study by a prominent consultant where it would become economic for a substantial and inefficient open circuit gas turbine (OCGT) component to be available for standby duties[5]. We have a situation where colossal sums are to be spent at Government initiative without the scrutiny of the Public Accounts Committee, as the electricity consumer and not the taxpayer fund these sums. The oversight of this process is nominally done by Ofgem who lack the knowledge, experience and resources to monitor this technical expenditure and whose recommendations are subject to ministerial decision, in turn heavily influenced by statutory targets. This is a recipe for widespread misallocation of resources[6].

Inflated estimates of energy output are not the only distortion used to promote wind farms but also carbon saving estimates. Replacement for coal generation was widely assumed that has since become discredited by appeals to the Advertising Standards

Authority. Scientific concern has also extended to carbon release from peat sinks with wind farm projects being sited on peat moor land[7]. Further distortion arises from the habit of quoting so many households such schemes would serve. This calculation introduces fudge factors so as to make it almost meaningless. Any estimate of energy output should be stated in megawatt-hours (MWh), nominally over an annual period. This re-introduces the question of load factor that has been shrouded in so much confusion and will be explored in Chapter 4.

Summary

Many uncertainties surround investment into much needed nuclear and coal technology, where without new build the generation mix will become lopsided. With the distortion of generous subsidy for renewable development and political preoccupation to meet EU renewable targets, a very real possibility exists of further delayed decision in crucial areas of investment. This will lead to an eleventh-hour commitment to gas turbine technology with its short constructional time-scales but longer lasting financial consequences.

Notes and References
1.   Ofgem Consultation of 9/10/2009 page 41 Ref 122/09.
2.   *The Guardian* 16 Aug 2009. *Energy experts call for carbon capture scheme for gas fired power stations.*
     http://www.guardian.co.uk/business/2009/aug/16/carbon-capture-gas-power-generation
3.   *Framework for the development of clean coal* – September 2009. Joint institutional submission http://www.theiet.org/publicaffairs/ submissions /sub836.pdf. http://www.profeng.com/archive/archive+2009/2214/ 22140053.htm Superheated technology
4.   *Review of potential hydroelectric development in the Scottish Highlands. Electronics and Power.* Pages 339-346. (IEE journal). May 1979.
5.   Parsons Brinckeroff report Dec 2009 – *Powering the future* pages 69/70. Interestingly on pages 11/12 this report forecast existing generating

capacity will be halved from its current level by 2023 with demand seeing no significant change. From 2020 the rate of new plant build required to maintain adequate capacity would need to at least equal the highest rate historically achieved.
http://www.pbpoweringthefuture.com/

6. *Sunday Times* 3 Jan 2010. *Offshore wind programme of £100 billion.*
http://business.timesonline.co.uk/tol/business/industry_sectors/
natural_resources/article6973943.ece

7. *Carbon savings and wind power on Lewis* – October 2007.
www.swap.org.uk

3   Justification for Renewable Policy

Comprehension is lost for those who do not appreciate the distinction between capacity and energy.

There can be no doubt, with the scale of expense having to be committed in promoting a renewable agenda, that it would never have gone forward without generous subsidies being in place.

The cost of these subsidies to the consumer are far from being transparent and arise in a number of devious ways above any incentive for the developer. When this renewable capacity has to be largely replicated by conventional means, the measure of economic penalty involved has to be justified on a platform of public policy. This expense is exaggerated by the failure to integrate this commitment into the wider energy scene where private market resources of capital, manufacturing and skill are required to compete with subsidised investment, concurrent with unprecedented levels of generating capacity being withdrawn. This, when the economic climate is insecure and burdened with public debt.

Since the inception of the Renewable Obligation Certificate (ROC) system of subsidy from 2002, terms had been consistent if loosely applied as with hydro resource where plant was de-rated to qualify[1]. The year 2009 saw the introduction of banding for certain renewable technologies and, for a limited period, offshore wind becoming eligible for double allocation[2]. In addition the ROC scheme has been extended by ten years to 2037. The logic of promoting nuclear generation as a carbon free source is overwhelming and were the prospect of subsidy to become available any nuclear developer would justifiably postpone his decision. To restore a level playing field the only logical course of action is to remove subsidy from wind resource. Even this may not be sufficient to restore investor confidence unless the whole system of ROC subsidies becomes dismantled. The existing commitment by the electricity consumer is unsustainable, particularly in the light of recent events[3].

This justification for renewable policy cannot be confined to cost but must embrace security of supply, not just in the sense of promoting sufficient generation capacity of suitable mix and fuel source but the gamble taken by impressing the intended programme of intermittent generation onto an inherently unstable grid system. The scale of this programme is 14GW for onshore wind and up to 33GW for offshore wind by 2030 although only 14GW is considered feasible for 2020 by government policy[4]. To give some perspective the British Grid system peak demand is almost 60GW. Energy studies and climate change are specialised fields of study impacting on electricity supply where credible response can only be made by asking questions. Three areas suggest analysis:

Strategic

With increasing environmental regulation and decline of North Sea oil and gas reserves, fuel sources are to be procured from overseas to a level of dependency never previously experienced in our history. By intentionally inflating the cost of energy to give marginal advantage to competitors, our economic strength becomes denuded leading to higher real costs of energy from imported supplies. At a fundamental level the problem of energy is not so much with its provision as with its cost.

The superficial attraction in developing renewable energy is to obtain 'free' fuel, thereby reducing the need to import fuel from overseas. However, fuel cost is only one component among many that come together to determine a price for that technology resource. Furthermore, significant costs arise with intermittent resource that is not borne by the generation supplier. One of the most costly items arising from dispersed renewable technology is the expense of repair and maintenance. Lacking the efficiencies of scale at any one location, any breakdown with such low rated and fragmented technology introduces an issue of economic viability, certainly on a domestic scale and over the longer term. Existing subsidy arrangements perpetuate this inefficiency. There is an irony in reducing our import dependency on fuel yet the technology for utilisation has to be imported. Furthermore significant renewable development promotes the integration of the GB Grid system into the continental grid network with all the political implications for future EU integration and dependency on power supply from Europe.

Resource Poverty

The major world-wide issue today should be population explosion, particularly in the undeveloped world where competition for resources become so acute as to diminish living standards, creating instability and conflict. The consequences of climate change bear far more heavily on the undeveloped world. If transfer of wealth from rich nations to poor is to become a reality it is through the mechanism of climate change in funding sustainable reforestation and infrastructure projects with an emphasis on water supply.

The developed world is not immune to pressure on irreplaceable resources created by demand, introducing pricing volatility and foreign adventures to secure these resources. Immigration becomes a contentious issue, provoked by a stagnant or depressed economy. Underlying common sense would applaud the need for personal constraint in our everyday living habits where entreaties alone would be insufficient without a driving imperative.

Climate Change

Climate change is essentially a natural phenomenon that has always existed and will continue to do so with mankind having to adapt in order to survive. The imprint of man upon the natural world has been extensive and damaging with technology being only one of many causes. Population growth is another, more pervasive, reason. The extension of destruction and exploitation by man into climate change is of another league entirely where the issue has to be disentangled from natural longer-term processes and placed into proper perspective. It makes far better sense for resources to be applied to adaptation than mitigation given the intractable scale of the problem, time-scale and uncertainties. Manmade carbon dioxide (CO_2) emissions comprise only 4% of worldwide emissions, the remainder being derived from natural processes, eventually becoming absorbed into oceans and vegetation within a natural cycle. Further, CO_2 emissions are only one of the various greenhouse gases together with water vapour influencing global temperature. The question to ask is: to what degree and over what time-scale does man-made CO_2 emission influence climate worldwide? Scientific opinion on this issue is deeply divided, compromised by political agendas that control funding for climate research, a relatively new field of study, heavily embroiled in computer modelling. Of late these techniques have not shone with glory as derivatives in banking were similarly processed and this in a field where the market imperative was prominent.

In accepting CO_2 emission reduction as an obligation, the next stage is to prioritise the steps leading to reductions by economic analysis for favoured options. Much would depend upon the time-scale and targets being chosen and not least the criteria of measurement. The standard of temperature rise, suggested as 2°C by the end of the century, is essentially symptomatic; sea level rise has an indisputable imperative with world-wide consistency, albeit of delayed response. For this exercise to be done in isolation from the international community is pointless and participants would naturally seek their own national advantage with such complicated discussions. Adjustments would arise based upon past emission contributions, developing status and economic damage. Compromise would become inevitable but of little consequence without penalties for non-compliance. All too easily, this process could descend into mutual suspicion, grandstanding and any rejection of failure. The casualty with such an outcome would be no rational process for worldwide emission reduction. The furore over leaked emails from the Climatic Research Unit (CRU) of East Anglia is to be welcomed. Its effect has been to question the science by removing the media mantra of 'settled debate' and allowing more open discussion for scientific inquiry that has been stigmatised in the past.

UK Commitment

Accepting CO_2 emission reduction as an obligation enshrined in EU directives, a stipulation of 20% emission reduction by 2020 has been implemented. The UK has negotiated an overall 15% figure for 2020 within this framework, choosing the lion's share to fall upon electricity generation as both heating and transport sectors are highly inflexible within the chosen time-scale[5]. Crucially, these targets have been entrenched into a statutory requirement to ensure civil service compliance, suggesting some hidden penalty for non-compliance of the agreed target. A motion introduced by the European parliament during 2008 calling for interim sanctions on a swingeing scale supports this proposition[6].

The rationale for the UK in choosing the share of reduction between heating, transport and power generation is crucial to comply with this EU commitment. With what technical scrutiny has this been determined and by what economic criteria? The suspicion exists that these proportions are decided upon political considerations of perceived public intrusion without any realisation of the unintended consequences that would follow. The unbelievable commitment to programme 33 gigawatts (GW) of renewable generation by 2020, regardless of constructional and technical feasibility implicit in this target, is the culmination of a series of arbitrary processes that are essentially politically driven[7].

The EU has an interventionist agenda to rationalise the structure of energy supply and in the process would remove the ability for any member nation to have an independent capability. This integration has been considerably enhanced in the economic sphere by the success of Euro currency. The

Westminster government, bound by treaty commitment, would wish to exploit the undoubted renewable *potential* of the UK as a substitute for declining reserves of North Sea oil and gas. The nationalist administration of the Scottish Government has promoted an independence agenda by ingratiating themselves with Brussels over their renewable policy. The calculation with this whole political scenario assumes a successful scale of renewable resource exploitation, driven more by wishful thinking than practical realities. A parliamentary report by Innovation, Universities, Science and Skills Committee issued in March 2009 stated:

> The Committee was shocked to discover that engineering advice was absent, or barely featured, in the formulation of key Government policies, including eco-towns, renewable energy and large IT projects. Engineering advice should be sought early, before policy is agreed.

Alternative Scenarios

Many approaches can be taken to reduce CO_2 emissions where conservation and technology with energy use must rank high. One area is the promotion of air transport. Certain questions need answers:

- Can emissions stemming from air travel into the upper atmosphere be equated in their effects from power generation nearer to sea level?
- Can the quantity of food imported by air be justified and could this be regulated?
- Can regulation be modified to avoid excessive waste of rejected food?
- Is the scale of international tourism by air sustainable?
- Can short haul air travel be substituted by improved rail infrastructure?

There is no doubting the unpopularity with some of these measures for the public. When balanced against the critical state of power generation and its long-term consequence for future national competitiveness, there is a clear absence of joined-up thinking and failure with long-term strategy. The distortions arising from promoting renewable energy sources are extensive and largely unseen. Certainly, the non-technical majority could never fully grasp the issues. Their promotion has created profound uncertainty towards investment into meaningful and necessary generation technologies. The attempt to stimulate micro-generation at a domestic level is fraught with technical issues of compatibility and exposure to commercial opportunism with short-term perspective. Sadly this approach also infects larger corporations where subsidy and regulation are rampant and money is to be made from such confused policy.

There is no better example of this mindset than so-called 'Smart Metering'. The policy to introduce power consumption information for both consumer and supplier is a hidden means for a future disconnection strategy to enable demand control, a measure made necessary by the increasing intermittence of renewable generation, where conventional generation alone has become recognised as being insufficiently responsive. What is galling for the consumer is that facility for power consumption information can be purchased for little over £10 from retailers to monitor individual appliances, information denied with its more sophisticated cousin. Furthermore the facility for remote metering also introduces the prospect of remote disconnection, an issue having profound social concern. This policy raises a range of questions:

- Would there be any choice to deny such installation?
- Would this metering be on a cheaper tariff?
- Would this disconnection be for the whole supply or for dedicated circuits? If dedicated circuits are involved this would involve considerable wiring adjustment on premises and additional equipment.

- How in practice could variable costing be monitored? What means of verification is there for the consumer? The scope for fraud could be high.
- How would liability for equipment be affected? Manufacturer's warranty may well be invalidated.
- Without dedicated circuits how would the Health & Safety issues be addressed?

Certain observations can be made:

- Consumer fatigue with volatile pricing would rapidly arise.
- Cost fluctuation varies considerably over the day, week, weekend and season so predetermining price access would be fraught with uncertainty and hazardous with food refrigeration.
- Predetermination by price requires dedicated circuits.
- It would be a very small step between disconnecting for necessity to safeguard the system and disconnecting for economic advantage.
- Initial parameters laid down at inception for frequency of disconnection would very quickly change with circumstance under duress.
- Most energy consumption relates to heating that is seasonal in character. This would not coincide with the period of intensive need for system demand control over the summer period.
- The economic imperative for remote metering is very strong for the supplier, suggesting this innovation is utility driven, quite independent of a requirement for system demand control.

At the end of 2009, Government announced a £9 billion programme for smart meters that for 26 million customers would average out at £350 for each household. Immediately following this announcement a warning from National Grid indicated consumers would end up spending billions of pounds on redundant smart metering technology if such devices were rushed through too quickly as the devices would not be able to communicate adequately with emerging 'smart grid' technology[8]. This spat illustrates the conflict between suppliers to access metering remotely and National Grid to deploy 'demand management' techniques (i.e. disconnection) to cope with increasing intermittence from wind development. Again, the cost would be borne by the customer and the question needs asking as to why the Government should be involved. There has clearly been no industry consultation by government.

These drawbacks would suggest the application of smart metering for domestic use would be inappropriate. The introduction of a third category of white meter tariff to cover the daily period 1630 to 1900hrs would provide generation capacity relief over the peak period of the day on a verifiable tariff. The incentive to adopt would relate directly to the chosen tariff giving the consumer choice of disconnection by timer switch for individual appliances. This approach would place responsibility for any disconnection where it belongs, with the consumer.

Sources of Information

Whatever policy the government decides, there should be credible technical advice available throughout the decision making process. All too often expertise is provided by commercial interests that are invariably aware that cost is not a predominant consideration. Repeated examples in government reports, certainly with the Scottish Executive, indicate insufficient understanding and lack of experience from the structure of civil service support. This deficiency does not appear to have been recognised and properly rectified.

Effective advice to formulate policy cannot be satisfactorily obtained from commercial organisations, however qualified by experience, without corresponding technical advice from appropriate impartial sources. The problem here is not so much the advice given as what is withheld. Academic advice without relevant industrial experience has to be qualified. Gaining information through consultation exercises can be effective as it can tap retired experts no longer constrained by institutional reprimand. Such an approach must have the confidence of those contributing. The call for evidence as administered by the House of Lords is conduct at its best. The acknowledgement of contributions is prompt, all submissions are published and hard copies of evidence and proceedings distributed. Government departments do not achieve this standard. There can be pressure for consultations to be done for cosmetic reasons which, from the perspective of the donor, undermines the whole exercise. Again, consultations can be directed for institutional response with individual submissions becoming ignored.

A most perplexing question is the role of professional institutions and the reasons why their technical expertise has not been more widely sought. Invariably, government has ignored many reports produced by such bodies. This can only promote apathy. Where information has been sought, there has been a selective approach towards academic sources who must be conscious of their future funding and lean towards what their client wishes to hear. Professional bodies are not immune from the interests of their members within profitable enterprises and a pervasive climate where conflict with any 'green' adversary with their missionary zeal would be prudently avoided. Another reason is that, within the narrow discipline of power engineering, knowledge and influence has become subsumed within an expansionist, commercially orientated, professional institution, trading standards for numbers.

Bureaucratic Comprehension

Confusion among public bodies is most common when distinguishing between capacity and energy, normally expressed as megawattt (MW) and megawatt-hour (MWh), an important distinction famously confused within the first annual report from Ofgem.

MW *represents a measure of energy capacity; MWh represents the time that capacity is exercised to give a quantity of energy. For most applications, these terms should be sufficient but can be extended.*

On occasion, a measure of capacity (MW) may be represented by mega volt ampere (MVA) as with transmission lines and transformers. In power terms they mean the same but allow for a reactive component (capacitive or inductive) increasing the current rating.

Summary

The crippling cost of developing uneconomic renewable resource has to seek public justification. The share allocated for the UK is in imbalance between the heat, transport and power generation sectors with unintended consequences. Political decision has disregarded technical and economic realities of application that should have been explored in the decision making process.

The conclusion one must reach is that renewable policy has become subservient to higher political objectives, suggesting a forced one-way dependence of national electrical supply upon continental sources where integration becomes an imperative to avoid Grid system instability.

Notes and References

1. Ofgem *1st Annual Report* page 35 para 5.10 also *Subsidies and Subterfuge* June 2005. www.swap.org.uk
2. ReNews 17/12/2009 Issue 182 page 11. The pre-budget report of December 2009 extended the period of double ROCs from the current year to a four year period. In addition the Greater Gabbard offshore scheme would now qualify. This change reversed an earlier announcement when the scheme had been authorised before the banding changes were introduced.
3. ThisisMoney 2 Jan 2010. *Regulator rethink over cost of green energy.* http://www.thisismoney.co.uk/markets/ article.html?in_article_id= 496767&in_page_id=3&position=moretopstories
4. BERR Consultation June 2008 page 11 para 31 & 32.
5. BERR Consultation June 2008 pages 6,7,8.

6. http://www.euractiv.com/en/energy/meps- give-major-boost-renewables-industry/article-175296?Ref=RSS   European Parliament briefing

7. *The Times* 18 Oct 2009. *E-ON condemns over ambitious targets for green energy.* http://timesonline-emails.co.uk/go.asp?/bTNL001/mDBLEMB/qDKL5MB/uUX984/xMQENMB

8. *The Times* 3 Dec 2009. *National Grid fears 'smart metering' being rushed.* http://business.timesonline.co.uk/tol/business/industry_sectors/natural_resources/article6941944.ece

4   Load Factor and Carbon Savings

Accepting the claims of a developer has all the understanding of a credit card commitment.

Load Factor

The importance of load factor cannot be overstated. It is defined as the ratio of actual energy produced (normally over an annual period) and the energy that would be produced were the generation source to run continuously. In short, its utilisation. Many factors arise to limit generation output; breakdown, maintenance, fuel supply and system requirements. This last item has many facets but primarily running costs determine choice of running for any generation supplier. Over 90% of operational generation is through bilateral contracts with up to 5% of energy exercised by National Grid over contracts covering their fluctuating role for system balancing[1]. Penalties for non-compliance are high, making the parameters within the financial trading system of critical importance to determine running choice.

Nuclear Generation has relatively low running costs with a low response capability making it well suited for baseload operation. Load factors of 90% and more are readily achievable although with ageing plant in the UK the incidence of breakdown has been rising. To extend operational life certain sites have effectively been de-rated by operating at reduced load[2].

Thermal Generation includes gas turbines, oil and coal fired generation, all competing as to whether they become part loaded, shutdown, on standby or taken out of service. Full load running achieves maximum efficiency to give the lowest running cost. Maintenance demands can be high and with fuel prices fluctuating, this sector is prone to becoming surplus for system requirements. Ageing plant is invariably least efficient, called upon less frequently thereby accelerating its final decommissioning.

Conventional Hydroelectric Generation has a surprising consistency of run-off over a full year, normally within a ten per cent range of long-term average. However, with many cascade schemes up to a year of run-off can be stored extending the range of annual load factor. Load factor is largely determined by design as a compromise between construction cost (where dam and tunnel civil works predominate), avoiding spill and system value for generation. Maintenance can invariably be timed over the summer months to avoid spill losses.

Wind resource load factor can reflect design but clearly optimises for maximum energy output with any specific location. Production is unpredictable and highly variable, typically producing variable power for about 80% of the time and achieving annual load factors averaging 26-27% across the United Kingdom[3]. The wind industry has in common use the term capacity factor instead of load factor but this is not a recognised international term and reflects American use[4]. It is best avoided as it can lead to confusion.

Load Factor determines output and therefore the viability for any investment. However, the structure of renewable subsidy is so generous, normal consideration with viability has been extended to such an extent as to cover almost any project. For wind resource, initial optimism by National Grid Transco promoted load factors of 35% as a GB average, leading to grossly inflated estimates for the scale of conventional plant that could be substituted. A figure of 20% of installed wind capacity was suggested[5]. This is known as *Capacity Credit* being a probabilistic figure defined as a percentage of installed wind capacity that can be considered as firm capacity for the purpose of plant scheduling. It is closely related to any given load factor in a non-linear relationship. Recent analysis has suggested a lower correlation derived from extensive winter anticyclones. In evidence to the House of Lords, one generation utility considered 8% to be an appropriate figure for the GB grid system[6].

Capacity Credit is important as contributing towards the total installed generation capacity available to meet peak demands on the grid system. Normally up to 20% '*capacity margin*' is required above peak system demands to cover contingencies for plant breakdown, demand estimation errors and other imponderables. In an absolute sense it could be argued that wind resource should have zero capacity credit because it is not dependable. As with so many other parameters connected with power supply statistical techniques are used to gauge an appropriate value that could be realistically adopted. Concern exists as to the extent that stable high-pressure cyclones could dominate winter weather patterns at the very time that peak demands for energy have to be met. This calculation has considerable implications for capital investment into alternative generation technologies.

Capacity or Plant Margin has been consistent over many years from the time of nationalisation but in that period the generation mix has changed completely. Not only has age introduced more unreliability in reaching its designed life of operation but a growing gas turbine component presents supply concerns that were not evident when coal used to be the dominant technology with large coal stocks being maintained at power stations. Around 20GW of gas turbine capacity is of similar design and operates close to its material limit creating a credible risk with generic type faults. The structure of the supply industry has also changed with pressure to reduce working capital, payment regimes that no longer reflect a capacity component and an increasing level of intermittence on the system. Significant retirement of coal and nuclear plant can be expected over this coming decade.

Considering wind resource development in the UK originated from the early 1990s, few statistics were available to establish load factor trends over the United Kingdom. It was not until March 2004 after the introduction of the ROC system of subsidy that a reliable indication of load factor became available based upon payment returns. Even as late as March 2006 figures produced by the then Department of Trade and Industry (DTI) presented UK average load factors of 29% and a 30% mean for Scotland over the period 1998 to 2004 with significant annual variations[7]. More recent analysis from ROC returns now reveals consistent UK annual averages nearer to 26-27%.

With hindsight, it should now be apparent the initial stimulus for wind development had been based upon a false prospectus with an exaggerated scale of output and inflated expectation of generation substitution, both revealed by depressed levels of load factor. It is self evident that corresponding claims for carbon savings also become affected.

Carbon Savings

The measures available for reducing carbon emissions vary from conservation with energy use and deforestation prevention to producing energy by renewable means. Economic analysis of the various measures indicate the latter to be the least cost effective, particularly with wind where quick fix mentality coupled to generous subsidy has created a serious obstacle towards investing in necessary and meaningful longer term technologies.

Carbon savings are a concept introduced when the concern with global warming became connected to carbon dioxide emissions. The Carbon Trust developed a fuel league table that listed the weight of carbon dioxide emitted to the burning of fuel, producing energy expressed in electrical terms. For example coal burning can be expressed as 780 grammes CO_2/kWh or even O.78 tonnes CO_2/MWh, both being identical but the latter expressed in scaled up units. As many forms of fuel contribute to electrical supply an inspired average was chosen (independent of efficiency conversion) of 0.43tonnes CO_2/MWh. This figure has remained constant since the millennium with the intention of review for 2010[8].

These calculations are arbitrary at best. Understandably, many variations are present from the calorific value (CV) of fuel to plant efficiencies over time with an improving mix of generation supply where updating inevitably lags well behind statistical returns. Developers in their calculations unsurprisingly would choose wind turbine output to substitute for coal equivalent carbon saving from electricity production, presenting exaggerated claims. This abuse was corrected in December 2005 by appealing to the Advertising Standards Authority who ruled that the overall conversion of 0.43 tonnes CO_2/MWh should apply. When combining reduced load factor to the corrected emission factor, claims for carbon saving in developers' submissions were readily halved.

Similar obfuscation arises with output relating to the 'number of households' any given development would serve. The variation as to what represents a typical household can only be imagined where 'adjustment' considerations arising from the nature of space heating in premises in proximity to a development would be gauged. The opportunity for distortion is obvious. Only the more reputable developers would give an annual energy output figure based upon MWh from which load factor could readily be calculated with installed capacity.

Using this technique in conjunction with ROC returns submitted to Ofgem enables a crude check to be made on the veracity of these ROC submissions. The temptation to manipulate must be strong with a state bureaucratic body lacking resources and practical technical support to police remote and dispersed locations. One noted inland wind farm site had a consistent load factor in excess of 40%. Load factor would also reveal significant breakdown problems.

Carbon saving has to consider loss of efficiency when operating a grid system where increasing levels of intermittence have to be accommodated from renewable generation. The issue is notoriously difficult to evaluate as so many parameters are involved. An inspired guess would suggest a 20% figure with standby or back-up plant where an increased commitment with warming up, idling, part loading and increased frequency of load changing is required. Ideally, thermal standby plant should be run continuously at steady full load for maximum efficiency; anything less introduces an avoidable proportionate increase in carbon emissions.

Recent analysis with GB grid balancing indicates the number of generation dispatches are in the proportions 45% for coal, 33% for gas and 16% pumped storage with an average 30 minute duration. These schedules are contract based and may not accurately reflect plant conditions. Adjustment for normal consumer demand variations also have to be separated from intermittence. Idling is a large component of carbon loss where with typical coal generation running at minimum load (quarter of full output) efficiency is reduced by a third. Combined cycle gas turbines (CCGT) are less responsive than coal. With increasing levels of intermittence, more plant has to be in a state of readiness by being kept warm for extended periods. Pumped storage has to consider the generation source for pumping as well as two-thirds efficiency with overall use. Cost, duration and plant responses are important considerations with scheduled choice for balancing. National Grid has on average almost fifty contract adjustments each hour that speaks volumes for the way plant is being operated[9].

Summary

Load factor is a crucial yardstick to monitor any generation investment but must relate to the resource in question. Load factor for renewable resource bears a close relationship with capacity credit and its influence on generation substitution. This has an effect when maintaining satisfactory plant margins for peak generation requirements. Load factor also enables inadequate substitute yardsticks to be better evaluated and allows a more accurate assessment for imprecise carbon saving calculations. Renewable generation has to have standby support that comes with increased carbon penalties.

Notes and References
1. UKERC. *The Costs and Impacts of Intermittency* – Imperial College March 2006 Item 2.2.3
2. British Energy sale prospectus – November 2008 page 137
3. Statistics available from DUKES (Digest of UK Energy Statistics). Similar values (if slightly less) are obtainable from the CLOWD ROC register website based upon ROC returns
4. International Electrotechnical Commission (IEC) with International Electrotechnical Vocabulary (IEV) of over 20,000 terms includes load factor but not capacity factor
5. House of Lords *Inquiry into the Practicalities of Renewable Energy* – Evidence by National Grid Transco of October 2003 page 49 para 35
6. House of Lords *Inquiry into the Economics of Renewable Energy* – Evidence by E-ON UK of June 2008 page 119 para 10
7. DTI Energy Trends of March 2006 – *UK Onshore wind capacity factors 1998-2004*
8. Carbon Trust conversion factor website. http://www.carbontrust.co.uk/cut-carbon-reduce-costs/calculate/carbon- footprinting/pages/2-types-carbon-foot-print.aspx
9. National Grid consultation. *Operating the Transmission Networks in 2020* – Chap 7 page 46. http://www.nationalgrid.com/NR/rdonlyres/32879A26-D6F2-4D82-9441-40FB2B0E2E0C/35116/Operating in2020 Consulation.pdf

5   Subsidy

When dishonesty brings high rewards and low penalties, crime is likely. When complacency is added it becomes a near certainty.

The United Kingdom is obliged to implement its share of a European Union target for carbon dioxide (CO_2) emission reduction of 20% by 2020. The UK share was negotiated to just 15% choosing to exercise most reduction on power supply from electricity generation. The general popular national expectation was that renewable forms of energy would become a substitute for the rapidly ageing stock of coal fired generation, largely constructed over the decade from 1965. Renewable power being uneconomic, it therefore became necessary for development to be induced by a levy. A system was created known as the Renewables Obligation, administered by Ofgem, where a certificate is issued for each megawatt-hour (MWh) produced, regardless of the renewable technology employed[1]. Although initiated by government, the electricity consumer and not the taxpayer would pay this levy that effectively would bind future administrations until 2027. This arrangement denies any investigation with audit from Public Accounts procedures. The scheme was introduced in 2002 but not until 2004 would the first annual figures become available as almost a full year elapses before the annual report is issued.

By January 2007 Ofgem had decided that the estimated cost of the scheme, £32 billion over a 25-year lifetime, was too expensive and that it should be reformed[2]. The Royal Society of Edinburgh with their Inquiry into Energy Issues for Scotland went even further in their opposition and stated the Renewables Obligation Certificate

(ROC) scheme should be replaced as soon as possible with a carbon emission reducing measure such as a carbon levy[3].

Incentive for the developer, covered by the Renewables Obligation, is only one component of the charges to exploit renewable resource that electricity consumers face. By 2010 this levy is expected to reach £1 billion per annum with an estimate on consumer bills at eight per cent of total, expected to rise sharply over this coming decade[4]. By October 2009, four gigawatts (GW) of wind resource had been connected with a government target for 33GW of renewable generation programmed by 2020. When instituted in 2002 the scheme was intended to last until 2027. In 2009 selective increase of this subsidy was introduced for marine renewable resource with offshore wind having a double allocation of certificates over a four-year period. Furthermore, the Renewables Obligation scheme was to be extended until 2037. There is no transparency of cost for electricity consumers over these arrangements.

In addition to what is a subsidy for the developer, there are other more onerous components of charges that over time will filter through to the consumer as a consequence of renewable exploitation:

Transmission. By their nature renewable resource is dispersed over sparsely populated regions requiring not just connection but extensive transmission reinforcement. An example of this is the £360M Beauly/Denny transmission project across the central Highlands of Scotland. These assets are not fully exercised for most of the time when connecting low utilisation renewable resource.

Constrained off Payments. To accommodate renewable connection, existing networks are exploited as far as possible, reducing their ability to absorb maintenance commitments with outages to accompany any new development. Where transmission constraints arise, generation sources are unable to export their power and therefore require appropriate compensation. In 2009 Highland wind farm projects totalling

450MW were given premature consent to connect with Ofgem approval on a connect and manage basis in order to promote government renewable targets[5]. Ofgem had previously estimated constrained off payments for 2009 would reach £262m, mainly from Scotland. This expense arises mostly for work upgrading border transmission circuits to allow additional exports from impending development of Scottish renewable resource, primarily wind[6].

Operational Accommodation. With increasing intermittence from renewable generation, mostly embedded into distribution networks, additional standby contingency must be made available from suitably responsive generation, coal fired being the most appropriate. This implies part-load operation, extended warming periods and more frequent generation dispatch. These costs are substantial and their carbon footprint should be debited against the renewable resource being accommodated. Further costs arise from technical standards of operation required under the transmission Grid codes.

Standby Generation Investment. The circumstance of intermittence that attends increasing renewable resource demands an almost similar capacity of standby generation having an appropriate response capability. The investment criteria for providing this capacity demands sufficient running to recoup this investment. With any scale of renewable resource, the opportunity for operational running is restricted and therefore some means of alternative funding becomes necessary to allow investment.

Nuclear Investment. Emerging consensus for essential development of nuclear generation recognises additional support will be necessary if investment is to proceed. To subsidise only renewable sources is plainly illogical, as capacity has to be largely replicated by fossil sources. Either all subsidies should be withdrawn or both should become eligible for support becoming a Low Carbon Obligation. The present arrangement is unsustainable, as predictable subsidy has been compromised and a level playing field must be restored, otherwise developers will not invest with such degree of uncertainty and prospect of lucrative subsidy.

Of the two options only the first is realistic. The scale of consumer support is already unsustainable with highly dubious justification, penalising the energy poor. The lack of transparency and cavalier approach by government to meet targets, regardless of expense, is on an upward leading trajectory that cannot be sustained in a climate of financial stringency and increasing public doubts over the case for climate change mitigation. The contortions of political posturing based upon fear only undermine the credibility of the case to support such extravagant and ill-conceived measures, having a long gestation, largely symbolic and futile in proportion to the global scale of the perceived problem.

This assessment of the current political environment has to be considered in the light of unfolding events that will galvanise public opinion in years to come. Escalating fuel bills inflated by misconceived subsidy can only provoke public resentment.

Financial Constraint. Recent financial turmoil has impoverished state finances with the triple effect of banking support, recession and reduced income receipts. This scale of unprecedented peacetime debt having to be repaid will lead to a severe contraction of state infrastructure investment and public service employment. Combined with the scale of consumer indebtedness, increased taxation and insecurity, the pressure to limit household expenditure will become intense.

Climate Change. Recent global cooling has cast doubt in the public mind about the justification for carbon mitigation policies, given their high cost and impact on energy supply.

Lack of Transparency. No attempt has been made to apportion the cost of renewable support subsidy onto consumer energy bills, least of all with commitment for infrastructure development and operating penalties.

System Security. The level of increased intermittence from wind development, the retirement of significant generation capacity through age, regulatory constraint and increasing dependence upon gas supply will all contribute towards a reduction of security of supply. There are also technical issues to be covered in the following chapter.

Summary
The political structure has become notorious for committing to unsustainable targets with little technical or practical understanding of the issues involved. The Climate Change legislation of 2009 setting targets for 2050 is a prominent example. Increasingly, regulation introduced from Brussels directives for mitigation has costs out of all proportion to the perceived benefit. The international preoccupation over global warming concern is inflicting such economic damage as to destabilise the very structures needed to fund security and future well-being. Cheap energy lies at the very heart of wealth creation whose inflated cost is as devastating with its effects as the suffocating taxation we are set to endure.

References
1. House of Lords Inquiry – *The Economics of Renewable Energy* – Nov 2008. Report page 88 Appendix 9.
2. *Reform of the Renewables Obligation 2006: Ofgem's response.* Ref 11/07 January 2007.
3. Royal Society of Edinburgh. *Inquiry into Energy Issues for Scotland* – June 2006. Recdn 20.
4. House of Lords Inquiry – *The Economics of Renewable Energy* – Nov 2008. Report page 61.

5.   Ofgem press release R/21 of 8/5/2009 – *Connection of 450MW low carbon generation*.

6.   Ofgem letter 17/2/2009 – *Managing constraints on GB Transmission System*.

6   Technical Realities

Give a dog a bone and it will be gnawed. Give a man a bone and it will be given to the dog.

In 2008 the Department of Business, Enterprise and Regulatory Reform submission to House of Lords Inquiry on Renewable Energy stated: 'The indications from National Grid and our own advisers are that there is no technical barrier to the connection of renewable generation at, for example, a 40% penetration level. The indications are that the challenge is an economic rather than technical one.' In reading this and the following chapter the reader should make a judgement on the veracity of this statement[1].

The intermittence of renewable resource has the potential to destabilise the Grid System. No defined level has ever been proposed, only the level at which significant cost would be incurred.

The analysis conducted within *Appendix 2* indicates this level of cost has long since been overtaken. No technical report has been published on this issue, only an academic international comparison, noticeably averaging all studies, mainly academic, without distinction from more experienced and practical sources[2]. Repeated reports refer to ongoing studies.

The sudden awareness of a problem with instability presents a seismic circumstance of unthinkable consequence. Assurances of technical accommodation contain caveats with open-ended cost implications and divided responsibilities. This problem is not an area for research but one of experience not readily quantified, and confined to the GB Grid system, circumstance with other grid systems being different. As is inevitable with any top driven approach, sustained by commercial interest, areas of uncertainty are sidelined, to await evidence, with the dangerous assumption in time of their being no problem of outstanding concern. With such a scenario, only events can provide the necessary evidence, making the inadequate response from the two grid incidents discussed in the next chapter of profound disquiet.

From an experienced standpoint and with the benefit of hindsight the level of knowledge and experience available within the structures of government relating to electrical power supply has been inadequate. As a consequence a number of failures can be identified:

- The failure to maintain an ordered succession of nuclear power stations.
- The lack of consistency in the structure of market conditions for generation scheduling.
- The near collapse of British Energy as a supplier of nuclear generated electricity.
- The disposal overseas of an indigenous capability for nuclear expertise in construction.
- The unbridled use of North Sea gas for power generation.
- The unsustainable scale of commitment for wind resource development.
- The absence of any body responsible for power supply, being left for market forces to resolve.
- The absence of any structure for long term planning of generation for security of supply.
- The assumption that power supply can absorb the brunt of optimistic carbon savings for 2020.

These items are all decision failures by government and their advisors over two decades that should never have happened and contain severe hidden economic penalties. This legacy is in sharp contrast to the stewardship exercised by the nationalised authority set up in post war years to meet unprecedented increases in demand. The transition from coal as the primary fuel for energy use into alternative technologies provided the single most effective advance in national health and well-being since vaccination. Another achievement is the scale of distribution cabling in our urban scene, overhead connection being common with so many of our continental neighbours. This is not to suggest a return to nationalisation would cure all our ills but it does reveal none of the above calamities would have happened were a single unified organisation in place, responsible for power generation and bulk transmission. Even with vertical integration of several companies, this cohesion would be unlikely.

The starry eyed obsession by all levels of government to promote renewable development is another manifestation of the same failure, driven by academic reasoning without corresponding practical experience. All too often schemes are developed, not by their potential for future viability but as a revenue source with continued and excessive subsidy, stimulated by the need to meet unrealistic politically driven targets. Moreover, the real damage lies with the failure to promote much needed investment into conventional technologies that are trammelled by regulatory hurdles and promoted by the self-same stargazers. The combination of commercial acquisitiveness with political naivety over subsidy has created the most dreadful mess that will reverberate for decades.

Micro-generation

A prominent field of green enthusiasm relates to micro-generation encouraging individuals to invest in generation on a domestic scale. Conservative Party energy policy will promote this misguided approach by further subsidy (*Appendix* 5C). Following the rhetoric of uninformed politicians and naive environmentalists, prospective purchasers investigating the practical implications with any purchase would find a range of obstacles to deter their commitment. The most obvious would be cost of purchase relating to pay-back time, although it must be said existing government policy is set to ramp electricity prices to levels that would dismay consumers. Another is neighbour intrusion where micro-wind generator suppliers have come to grief with unacceptable noise levels and insufficient running within an urban setting. A less obvious hurdle has been various tariff structures by utilities that do not encourage back feeding of supply into the distribution network. Such policy is sound as safety risk from localised disconnection and transient interference is best avoided.

Capital outlay for projects is usually significant, only becoming worthwhile for schemes involving heat pumps where land is available or on a new construction. Any subsidy would be seen as socially selective. Unless photo-voltaic costs can be significantly reduced, scope for domestic energy supply from this form of micro-generation source would not be viable, particularly in northern climes with such limited winter solar exposure.

What does undermine all domestic micro-generation schemes are unknown and onerous servicing costs where specialised skilled personnel travelling large distances have to service dispersed small generation units with a multiplicity of components having limited shelf-life replacement. This expense is not exposed in project analysis but is crippling for the viability of many schemes over the longer term. Being a variable and random cost, it is often conveniently ignored. In storm conditions these schemes are highly susceptible to tripping with power surges from faults. Micro-generation cannot be expected to comply with Grid Codes and the incidence of failure with any faults would remain unknown, such are the logistical realities. Any extensive deployment of micro-generation presents an increased level of intermittence from distribution networks that must be centrally accommodated at additional expense. It is not widely appreciated that network losses arise mainly within lower voltage distribution systems and not from bulk transmission on the national Grid system.

Intermittence

The scale of intermittence to be accommodated is daunting given the level of intent. Few professionals can say never but privately in conversation many do. Currently it is the response capability with generation that must cope with the vicissitudes of combined consumer demand and intermittence from renewable sources. Although accommodating measures can mitigate extremes it is not sufficient to accept 99% success as the 1% failure is where the damage is done. This position has been recognised with proposals for demand management and expanded continental interconnection to support existing arrangements.

Demand Management has already been implemented to a limited extent with industrial consumers, on a reduced tariff for accepting disconnection, subject to notice. Certain tariffs such as white meter have differential rates for fixed periods of the daily cycle that cannot be changed but do influence customer choice with demand. Some tariffs have been introduced for space heating where control is by radio signal on a predetermined basis. In extremis and with notice this may be adjusted but its efficacy is related to the season. Proposals have been aired to widen the scope among domestic consumers to cover items such as refrigeration, electric car servicing and water heating by direct disconnection on an instantaneous basis using the mains cable to effect control by superimposed frequency signals or alternative mobile phone technology. These options present a number of hidden complications. If such disconnection were appliance-orientated would manufacturers accept full warranty? Interruption of car battery charging could be problematic. If circuit selection was intended, unless it was a new installation, extensive rewiring and terminal facilities would be needed. Who would pay for modification when the benefit is for grid balancing with necessary adjustments and tariffs routed through the local supplier? Inevitably, customers would require some form of compensation or incentive to accept even limited disconnection. Fuel poverty is set to become much more of an issue and if a whole supply could be disconnected, it would provide a means of subsidy for those in less fortunate circumstance.

The euphemism for 'smart metering' disguises a strong economic imperative for suppliers (who are now termed

Distribution Network Operators or DNOs), to access metering remotely. While variable costing sounds an attractive concept for the customer, it could easily founder with the problem of verification, consumer fatigue with the vicissitudes of pricing and the cost for providing selected access to appliances with any pre-selection in mind. Health concern over refrigeration could arise. As for consumption information, this can readily be obtained with a plug-in handset from retailers at a fraction of the cost with the advantage of selective use. More benefit for the Grid operator can be gained by introducing a third category with the white meter tariff to cover the daily evening peak period, enabling a reduced scale of generation commitment.

However there are other risks for the consumer that attends demand management. It is a very small step between disconnection to ensure Grid security and disconnection for economic advantage with Grid operation. Any safeguards with parameters to limit disconnection, introduced at inception, would rapidly change under duress. Were this facility also extended to disconnection of supply for non-payment in conjunction with remote metering, some very serious social issues would arise. In conclusion, the concept of smart metering for demand management would not be appropriate for the domestic consumer although its use with the commercial and industrial sectors would have an application.

Continental Interconnection would alleviate concerns over intermittence to some degree but could not provide any absolute assurance as such trading would be by mutual consent. The GB Grid system could not be integrated by alternating current (AC) connection to the Continental system so would retain its operating status as a separate entity. It can be foreseen that with escalating generation costs a tendency for importing would arise with the trading opportunities presented. To accommodate intermittence, the facility has to be available in both directions and would need to be very substantial in scope to accommodate the scale of wind resource introduced by government policy. Much interconnection could be influenced by offshore wind production on a variable basis and technically this fluctuation is best accommodated at the continental end although commercial reality would indicate the opposite. This is what an offshore grid would have to accommodate. A revealing snippet from a trade journal indicates 80% of offshore insurance claims are cable related[3].

Danish experience does not encourage such extensive offshore wind development. Much of their own wind production has to be sold to neighbouring system operators at depressed prices, even at negative pricing, because this production coincides with significant north German wind capacity.

Danish export can be readily absorbed by two fortuitous circumstances: a significant interconnection of transmission with all its neighbours and a predominance of responsive hydro generation capacity in Norway and to a lesser extent in Sweden[4].

Offshore wind production from the North Sea only exacerbates this situation as experience shows the level of output from wind encompasses large areas with passing weather systems, undermining the claims of wind protagonists for offsetting dispersion. The implication of this scenario would deter exporting at depressed prices, if it was feasible for North Sea offshore wind to become absorbed onto the GB Grid system, this at a time when remaining national wind capacity would be generating. The outcome becomes obvious: significant commercial pressure would induce excessive absorption of wind output on the GB Grid system requiring a dependency on standby plant and *force majeure* imports once wind subsided. Such conditions would coincide at the very time when grid system operation is most vulnerable, during winter storms or summer gales. This is not the way a Grid system should be operated, something that will be explored in the next chapter.

The vulnerability of undersea cable cannot be discounted. Although breakdown seldom happens, when it does, extended periods are needed for location and repair, particularly under marine conditions. Sophisticated techniques in the hands of terrorists would create a significant security problem. But it does not need terrorism to expose the vulnerable condition of system control where constant correction is needed to maintain system balance, aggravated by intermittence. Reliable widespread communication links are essential, which, together with highly computerised techniques, create a worryingly high degree of technical sophistication that must have instant response at all times.

Under these scenarios the GB Grid system becomes hostage to fortune. Since privatisation, the role of National Grid has been emasculated from disciplined control of the whole network to a niche accountability confined to system balancing and owner of transmission assets in England and Wales, without any generation responsibilities apart from accommodation. No overriding technical authority exists. This adventure into wholesale intermittence, smart metering and micro-generation can only end in tears.

Scheduling of Generation presents a hidden problem in coping with intermittence. It is crucial for the stability of the Grid system that means to cope with intermittence are fully robust. Comparison can be made with the scale of demand excursion being successfully accommodated; this assumes similar events from intermittence would also be satisfactorily managed. Such an assumption would be false, as the nature of both requirements is different. Significant demand excursions are invariably predictable in scale and timing, intermittence events are much less so with the added complication that they can move in either direction. This condition prevents any anticipatory action with slower moving generation plant. Once pumped storage reserves are committed, response capability with remaining reserve is less certain and subject to time delay.

Another related concern is with the conditions attached to balancing contracts that may not mirror actual performance. Any generation supplier would wish to maximise his return as well as buttressing his commitment. These comments are of course conjectural where commercial confidentiality restricts information. The incidence of scheduling adjustments is also becoming an issue where rising frequency to cope with increasing intermittence has a significant adverse non-linear relationship[5].

Currently, on average, almost fifty scheduling adjustments are made each hour with an average duration of about 30 minutes. These figures disguise the rate at peak intensity. Typically almost half of all adjustments relate to coal generation, a third for gas and a sixth with pumped storage. These changes exceed 400,000 a year, presenting an issue of maintenance and reliability, both with ageing coal plant and high performance gas turbines, all set on an accelerating trend. To cope with this intensity of dispatch, National Grid has proposed an automatic system of 'fly by wire' raising the question of what would happen under fault circumstance and effectiveness with a return to manual control.

With more sedate operation under nationalisation, the first line of correction with any variation of system frequency was governor response. This is an installed automatic feature with all synchronous generation plant that enables a limited correction to be given for restoration of frequency and is a continuous facility. Historically wind turbines have lacked this capability and although Grid Code changes introduced in the summer of 2005 now require this facility to be provided, it is not at all clear what scale of derogation (relaxation of standards) is involved. There is the consistency with implementing and the knowledge that wind farms less than 50 megawatts (MW) capacity in England and Wales are exempt (the ceiling for Scotland is lower). In addition, with privatisation, the facility of governor response has become a paid-for service giving a variable and unknown level of use, suggesting significant depletion of this facility. With limited call for wind farm response, it may be questioned how effective this facility may become when needed, particularly with the problem of inconsistent output across the area of a wind farm.

Command and Control. Robust dispatch is not confined to the response capability of generation plant but extends to the chain of command and control apparatus between control rooms. This comprises links for communication, computerised displays known as system control, alarms and data acquisition (SCADA), printers and telephone contact, all supported by non-interruptible power supplies. The reliability of such equipment is an essential part of the whole chain of circumstance to receive information and implement instructions where widespread communication links are an integral part to the whole process. Although back-up systems are commonplace, the sheer scale and complexity of equipment involved cannot remove the risk, however unlikely, of interruption.

Derogation

In 2005 the German utility E-On Netz was obliged to increase its spinning reserve from 60% to 90% of wind output capacity to overcome the effect of a postulated system fault, tripping out induction wind turbines on their system[6]. Subsequently the additional cost of this precaution came to be shared among all German utilities. Measures were initiated to overcome this problem of sympathetic tripping by replacement or modification. Replacement wind installations have double wound machines to limit this effect. At about the same time National Grid had modified their Grid Codes, stipulating all wind farms in England and Wales above 50MW to have facility for variable response with both frequency and voltage conditions (in Scotland the threshold is 30MW in the south and 10MW for the Highlands). Increasingly offshore wind is set to become a major component of wind resource. In June 2009 National Grid became the transmission system operator (TSO) for the developing offshore grid that together with the onshore GB Grid system will become known as National Electricity Transmission System (NETS). The more familiar GB Grid system term is used throughout this book. The threshold for Grid Code compliance offshore is 10MW[7].

Responsibility for ensuring compliance rests with the transmission owner being National Grid for England and Wales above 100MW capacity. Between 50 and 100MW capacity, compliance is undertaken by the DNOs[8]. The profile of the GB Grid system precludes any direct Grid connection of onshore wind except for Scotland where most capacity is Grid connected at 132 kilovolts (kV). Clearly capacity was connected and under construction before the new Grid Codes came into force.

In the UK there has been no comparable programme of replacement as undertaken in Germany. Inevitably, there must be significant capacity that has derogation in addition to non-qualifying capacity. The gravity of this problem was given in evidence to the 2004 House of Lords inquiry by National Grid when, 'without an acceptable technical solution, the effect of sympathetic tripping could seriously limit the number of wind turbines that could be accommodated[9].' With 47GW of intended wind resource announced in 2009, a rigorous examination of all aspects pertaining to this question is urgently required.

It is salutary to know in Germany there is a very substantial programme of wind turbine replacement, raising the suspicion where these second hand machines will eventually be used. One of the principal recommendations arising from the continental grid incident of November 2006 was that, 'the requirements for frequency and voltage variations of generation units connected to the distribution grid to be the same in terms of behaviour as that of units connected to the transmission network, becoming retrospective'[10].

The practical knowledge of wind integration studies by Union for the Co-ordination of the Transmission of Electricity (UCTE), the Danish Eltra and German E-On Netz utilities, all provide relevant insights into the technical problems associated with levels of wind resource, far in excess of UK experience. The problem with sympathetic tripping still exists to a degree; this, and other technical inadequacies have been highlighted in October 2009 with an application by National Grid for derogation of substantial offshore wind capacity under operation and construction[11]. The question arises just how much wind turbine capacity on the GB network is fully compliant with the GB Grid Codes?

Embedded Generation Frequency Settings

In the early part of 2008 National Grid circulated an appeal to all DNOs to establish the high frequency settings and scale of embedded generation where it was suspected settings were set much lower than for grid connected generation. This appeal recognised that significant uncertainty existed with up to 6GW of embedded generation that, if triggered, could present a system risk of disconnection. Six months was given to evaluate the scale of the problem: considering the number of units affected, the knowledge that this issue had been flagged four years earlier and the size of potential loss, evident concern arises whether this exercise has been fully evaluated. What compulsion to comply exists and how effective are current arrangements? This issue does reveal a structural weakness where no overriding technical authority is in place.

There are fourteen electricity distribution networks (DNOs) owned by seven companies from whom this information must be sought. This circumstance extends to notification of generation tripping with any Grid transmission fault. The scale and complexity of this process becomes a logistical nightmare lacking consistency and given the absence of rigour to enforce compliance, a circumstance of neglect becomes inevitable, extending to other fields of inquiry.

Accelerated Connection

In the summer of 2009, Ofgem authorised the connection of 450MW of wind resource in the Scottish Highlands constrained by transmission capacity. This measure was promoted through the Transmission Access Review consultation to remove obstacles preventing the promotion of renewable targets. This relaxation represented almost half the capacity of installed hydroelectric generation in the region[12]. An inevitable consequence will be accelerated compensation payments for generators whenever transmission constraints arise to prevent their output being exported. When so much wind capacity has already been connected, constraints arising with transmission and substation maintenance commitments will induce a high level of compensation. Cost apart, this measure has implications for operational control to ensure any hazard for circuit overload is avoided. It represents a further unwanted burden above all the difficulties with intermittence that control staff must accommodate above their normal duties.

Consumer Demand

The assessment for finding the level of consumer demand is based upon a zero sum calculation when all other parameters have been established. By introducing significant levels of embedded generation and micro-generation that are not monitored, the GB Grid system only sees a net value, making any real time assessment of actual consumer demand more uncertain over time. This unresolved issue would have increasing implications for system reinforcement and design.

Summary

Serious failings in energy policy are the result of a lack of technical appreciation and knowledge of practical constraints surrounding the various new technologies and a failure to benefit from overseas experience. Logistical restraints and an absence of overall technical authority have led to destabilising issues not being adequately addressed. In the absence of overall responsibility for system direction and performance, a credible circumstance of failure exists, given the high level of targeted wind resource.

References
1. House of Lords Inquiry – *The Economics of Renewable Energy* – Nov 2008. Evidence page 213.
2. UKERC. *The Costs and Impacts of Intermittency* – Imperial College March 2006.
3. ReNews 3/12/2009 Issue 181 page 14.
4. CEPOS – *Wind Energy – the case of Denmark* – September 2009. Part 1 page 6.
5. National Grid Consultation – *Operating the Transmission Networks in 2020*. Chap 7 page 50.
6. E-ON Netz *Wind Report 2005* page 4.

7. Ofgem Consultation 131/09 of 29/10/09 page 2.
    http://www.ofgem.gov.uk/Networks/offtrans/pdc/cdr/cons2009/
    Documents1/091029_offshore_derogation.pdf
8. Grid Code Compliance of large wind farms in the GB transmission
    system. A paper by Urdal and Horne of NGET.
9. House of Lords *Inquiry into the Practicalities of Renewable Energy* –
    Evidence by National Grid Transco of October 2003 page 49 para 31.
10. UCTE final report of system disturbance on 4 Nov 2006 page 61 recmdn 5
11. Ofgem Consultation 131/09 of 29/10/09 following National Grid
    application for derogation.
12. Ofgem press release R/21 of 8/5/2009 – *Connection of 450MW low
    carbon generation.*

7   Grid System Incidents

Imagination is more important than knowledge.

Albert Einstein

This chapter illustrates how deficiencies outlined in the previous chapter come to bear on actual events. The recommendations from the first incident of Grid failure on the continent have relevance for the second incident, where insufficient information has prevented the probable cause of disconnection with the second incident becoming known.

European Grid Failure

On 4 November 2006 in Germany a short duration outage was approved to allow the passage of a cruise liner along the Ems River. A succession of events led to widespread disconnection of supply across continental Europe. Details of the incident and comment by the author made at the time are given in *Appendix 3A*.

The scale of wind resources, while not the direct cause of the incident, had a material effect on restoration and had previously given rise to uncontrolled flows in certain parts of the European transmission network. It is clear from the E-On Netz report that the transmission system was being run at its upper limit to accommodate power transfers across the continental network, leaving little headroom for contingency. The background to this incident presents the dilemma facing operators when commercial pressures conflict with prudent operation. The knowledge of previous outages having been successfully managed only increases the likelihood of failure, a phenomenon usually known as Russian Roulette.

The lessons to emerge for the GB Grid system are in the recommendations that were made in the UCTE final report[1]. To quote recommendation 5:

The regulatory or legal framework has to be adapted in terms of the following aspects:

1. Transmission System Operators (TSO) should have the control over generation output (changes of schedules, ability to start/stop the units)
2. Requirements to be fulfilled by generation units connected to the distribution grid should be the same in terms of behaviour during frequency and voltage variations as for the units connected to the transmission network. These requirements should be applied also to units already connected to transmission and distribution grids.
3. Operators of generation units connected to the transmission grid must be obliged to inform their TSO about their generation schedules and intra-day changes of programmes prior to their implementation.
4. TSOs should receive on-line data of generation connected to DSOs grids (at least 1-minute data)

Observations
a) A significant amount of generation tripped from frequency disturbance on the distribution systems, notably wind turbines.
b) The importance of generation schedules for the TSO is the risk of having improper system security assessments.
c) Even on their own transmission systems certain TSOs could not control wind generation.
d) Restoration of supply was inhibited by the scale of uncontrolled embedded generation.
e) Real time data was not available to monitor what power was being generated on the distribution networks.

This omission has several consequences:

No real time knowledge of total national balance between supply and demand.

No real time knowledge of generation started on distribution networks and possible tripping/reconnection in the event of frequency or voltage drop.

No real time knowledge of generation started up on distribution networks and possible impact on grid congestion on the HV Grid System.

To the author's knowledge, of the above items 1 and 4 are not implemented on the GB Grid system and item 3 is uncertain but probable. Were recommendation 4 in force with the second grid incident to be discussed, many uncertainties would have been resolved. It is with item 2 where significant departures exist on the GB Grid system with much wind capacity not being covered by the Grid Codes and the scale of derogation unknown.

The continental incident was not catastrophic, as the splits into component parts were sufficiently large with independent control to prevent collapse. The period of delay before achieving a unified system restoration was impressive given the scale of disruption. The GB Grid system does not have the inertia of the continental system and only a single controlling authority, making any parallel incident on the GB system likely to be of much longer duration in making any restoration.

GB Grid Failure

On the morning of 27 May 2008 losses of generation within five minutes were on such a scale as to initiate the tripping of low frequency relays, disconnecting an estimated 550,000 consumers. This automatic corrective feature is the final graded response to prevent system collapse. Comment by the author is made in

Appendix 3B relating to a report produced after this incident although a second report was produced nine months later[2].

Both reports are unconvincing and fail to examine the entirely credible alternative of a wind excursion that prompted final disconnection of consumers. Only in the second report is this alternative even mentioned. With well over 2GW of installed uncontrolled wind capacity embedded into the grid network on a blustery day and the prevarication with identifying embedded generation from DNOs, both reports are deficient, not so much in what they say as with what has been omitted. The only wind resource monitored came from Scotland where capacity is connected at the grid voltage of 132kV. Attempts to establish wind performance from National Grid were not forthcoming. The reports revealed several issues of concern:

a) The scale of low frequency demand disconnection was exceptional as was the unusual extent of generation losses.

b) The scale of within day generation losses prior to the incident.

c) The limited extent of demand reduction realised by manual voltage reduction measures.

d) The vulnerability of embedded generation to trip with frequency excursions.

e) The inability to identify the mode of generation losses from DNOs.

f) The limited contribution from pumped storage plant.

g) The economic case to justify raising response and reserve levels for future incidents was discounted on the basis of financial loss to the supply industry. Consumer loss was disregarded.

Summary

The detached approach from embedded generation is at the very core in identifying the cause that finally led to disconnection. This issue is at the heart of what led the UCTE to recommend the measures they did with the first grid incident. *Appendix 2* contains the predictions of failure with both of these incidents. Were wind intermittence to be established as the cause of disconnection a fundamental review of operating procedures would become necessary at significant cost if implemented.

References
1. UCTE final report of system disturbance on 4 Nov 2006 page 61 recmdn 5
2. http://www.nationalgrid.com/NR/rdonlyres/E19B4740-C056-4795-A567-91725ECF799B/32165/Public FrequencyDeviationReport.pdf
   National grid investigation into disconnection of 27 May 2008 – issued February 2009.

8   When Will the Lights Go Out?

With those who spin the Emperor's clothes, it is not so much a matter of deceit as self-interest without principle.

The above cry has become a well-worn catch-phrase to highlight concern with the parlous condition of generation supply in the United Kingdom. It remains true and would appear to be the only way that politicians can become aware of a problem caused by their own neglect. Many a colleague with a touch of cynicism has said nothing will happen until the lights go out.

The concentration of government effort to promote a renewable agenda has introduced significant uncontrolled and unpredictable generation capacity onto the GB Grid system. This intermittence is potentially destabilising and measures to mitigate this increasing problem are extremely expensive. Even were this policy to be revoked, sufficient capacity under construction would present a continuing problem that would need compensating mitigation.

The grid incident of 27 May 2008 was not caused by one single failure but by a combination of generation losses that was highly unusual involving the most severe single event loss for which the grid system is designed to manage. The scale of this loss had not been experienced for ten years and was the third statutory reportable frequency deviation since privatisation. This incident was the only one to trigger consumer disconnection by low frequency relays. Over a score of plant losses in excess of one gigawatt (GW) have been experienced over the last ten years.

The point to be made is that contingency cannot cover all eventualities where more than one incident becomes involved. It is the supervention of intermittence from uncontrolled wind resource that becomes the joker in the pack. Recognising the conditions for such excursions would coincide weather-wise with additional hazard from transmission fault and generation loss. Furthermore a circumstance is rapidly developing where spurious micro-generation and embedded distribution plant tripping would provide further generation loss from any incident, provoked by system disturbance as was experienced on 27 May.

Continental experience of wind excursions has shown swings of half the installed wind capacity in hourly time-scales[1]. For the UK with Atlantic exposure and offshore installation even higher values may arise. In October 2009, installed wind resource over the GB network was 4GW and government intent is to reach a 30GW target for 2020. The grid incident described had a total generation loss approaching 2GW. The well-publicised demand excursions from TV programmes can be in the order of 3.5GW but this must be qualified for wind intermittence as explained in Chapter 6. It must be remembered that frequency excursion that arises from loss of generation is proportionate to the total system demand at the time. This is why the loss of 1GW during a summer gale can have twice the impact as from a winter blizzard.

A number of informed professional engineers consider 10GW as a ceiling for wind installation onto the GB Grid system. The author considers 6GW as a more appropriate figure when problems with instability will start to become unmanageable (refer to *Appendix 4B*). At significant expense these limits may be raised by investment with interconnection and further demand management. More pumped storage may be considered but siting could be an issue. Essentially these measures seek to contain a problem that should never have arisen and become absurd when the resource in question is hopelessly uneconomic.

Coincident with rising intermittence is the accelerating balancing response that is already averaging almost fifty adjustments each hour, and this is an average. What rate is experienced at periods of peak intensity is unknown but clearly there is an increasing problem. The scale of derogation and embedded wind resource that do not comply with grid codes provide another concern where unacceptable sympathetic tripping could arise from any system fault. Sophisticated control techniques associated with demand management, generation scheduling and an offshore grid presents further concerns. Recent innovations and unprecedented levels of rising intermittence coupled with existing outdated (though still functional) infrastructure have created a new uncertainty. A judgement must be made as to when the risk of disconnection becomes too high. As is so often the case in commercial environments such boundaries are influenced by non-technical considerations as seen with the continental grid incident. Increasingly management culture has become more targeted on cost control and straitjacketed by rising regulation.

As if this witches' brew was not enough, further considerations will reduce security of supply. Leading up to mid decade, unprecedented levels of nuclear, oil and coal generation capacity will be withdrawn from service and increasing age and frequency of operation will reduce reliance and availability of remaining generation capacity[2]. Fuel options will be constrained, becoming more reliant on gas when North Sea supplies are rapidly declining. In the time scale available only gas turbine capacity can reliably be provided when coal should have been the logical choice. Ominously the scale of future electricity price increases would relieve this condition by reduced demand. The authoritative Parsons Brinckerhoff study referred to in the notes for Chapter 2 suggests existing generating capacity will be halved by 2023 with replacement capacity having to be built at a rate from 2020 to equal the highest historical rate ever achieved.

The cold snap of January 2010 revealed the shortcomings with energy supply when industry experienced widespread disruption of gas supplies, not entirely due to a temporary outage of a Norwegian gas pipeline. Generation output was 45% from coal, 37% from gas and 15% from nuclear with just 0.2% from wind. The declining availability from coal and nuclear capacity over this coming decade indicates the reliance being placed upon gas supply where domestic consumers take priority over industry and power generation. Any multinational organisation would not invest in the UK with such a vulnerable outlook over power supplies[3]. In fact the reverse is the case where the rising cost of fuel will see energy intensive industries migrating overseas in a global market.

But who is to take responsibility for this emerging crisis and who is to call time? There is no defined responsibility and strategic forward planning with electrical supply. Experience shows just how much confidence can be placed upon the structures of government. Even now the energy policies of all the main parties are inadequate, placing reliance on renewable resource above the proven nuclear and coal foundation that has served this nation so well in the past. To answer the question with the title of this chapter; all that can be seen ahead is a hole being dug when the government should have stopped digging years ago. Perhaps the cynics are right and the lights will have to go out before the politicians come on board.

Notes and references

1. On 28/29 Oct 2000 on the Danish Eltra system under storm conditions an hourly peak wind output of 1715 megawatts (MW) was preceded by 711MW. Following hourly output dropped to 951MW. As these were summated figures, actual values would differ. This suggests rates of 13-17MW/min.

    On 19 Nov 2003 E-ON Netz with an installed wind capacity of 6.25GW experienced a drop of 3.64GW over six hours, a rate of 10MW per min. On 24 Dec 2004 a drop of 4GW was experienced over ten hours with a peak rate of 17MW per min.

2. To illustrate the uncertainties with prediction, nuclear performance providing baseload energy from advanced gas-cooled reactor (AGR) power stations are taken. Table 1 indicates the scheduled closure dates for AGR nuclear power stations as given by British Energy in November 2008. Corresponding DECC estimates are given. Table 2 gives a declining energy output total for these stations over the previous five financial years. A total capacity of 7.5GW has provided between 14% and 10% of annual national electricity demand for energy over this period.

TABLE 1

	Capacity MW	Generation commenced	Scheduled Closure	DECC estimate
Hunterston B	820	Feb 1976	2016	2014-18
Hinkley Point B	820	Feb 1976	2016	2016-20
Dungeness B	1040	Apr 1983	2018	2016-20
Heysham 1	1160	July 1983	2014	2014-18
Hartlepool	1190	Aug 1983	2014	2014-18
Torness	1230	May 1988	2023	2023-27
Heysham 2	1235	July 1988	2023	2023-27

TABLE 2

	2003/4	2004/5	2005/6	2006/7	2007/8
Energy TWh	56.2	50.7	51.5	42.4	40.6
Load Factor	86%	77%	78%	65%	62%

3. Press report in the Guardian/Observer website of 10 January 2010. *UK power prepares for a cold wind of change*. http://www.guardian.co.uk/business/2010/jan/10/wind-energy-power-electricity

9   Beauly/Denny Public Inquiry

Those who ignore the lessons of the past are ordained to repeat them in the future.

Scotland is expected to absorb the major share of onshore renewable development and with numbers of dispersed planning inquiries in rural communities having limited professional backing and resources, developers have major advantages over objections from local communities. Once the interests of landowners are satisfied, only the objections of local authorities remain. However, even they are at a disadvantage if such areas of land do not have formal areas of conservation and historical interest. In addition, the cumulative costs of appeal is prohibitive. The scale and impact of the Beauly/Denny transmission application brought together three councils and National Park authority with numerous conservation bodies for objection. This 400kV transmission line passes through unspoilt landscape where tourism provides the major source of income for the local economy. The consequent public inquiry was the longest and most expensive that Scotland had experienced since devolution.

The author gave evidence (*Appendices 4A and 4B*) to this long running Inquiry held between 6 February and 11 May 2007 as one of two independent witnesses at the strategic session, working with other objectors and primarily the Beauly Denny Landscape Group (BDLG). This grouping comprised the John Muir Trust (the leading objector), National Trust for Scotland, Ramblers Association Scotland, Association for the Protection of Rural Scotland, Scottish Wild Land Group and Mountaineering Council of Scotland. Alone among the various objectors the BDLG had not advocated any under-grounding of the line as being an inadequate solution[1]. Sadly most objection was diffused by concentrating their opposition on mitigation by undergrounding.

The application was presented by Scottish & Southern Energy (SSE) and Scottish Power (SP) for a 136 mile-long 400kV transmission line between Beauly (ten miles west of Inverness) and Denny (eight miles south of Stirling) through some of the most evocative Highland landscape. The project, described as an upgrade when in reality a brand new construction, would replace an existing adjacent 132 kilovolts (kV) transmission line. The cost of the line was estimated at £253m with the overall project cost at £354m, the difference to allow for significant substation capacity at four locations in addition to the terminal points. Although being strung for 400kV operation, the second circuit would operate at 275kV in order to harvest wind resource along its route. This project enables exploitation of significant wind resource over the western Grampian Highlands, extending above the Great Glen.

Under strict rules of procedure, evidence could not be submitted once a precognition had been lodged. Objectors were in a position of considerable disadvantage with not knowing until the last moment the intended conditions and capacity of installation to be applied for, coupled to the sheer volume of supporting documents, all having to be distributed over the Christmas festive period. For these reasons, a detailed late submission by an independent witness, who had been responsible for the design of the existing transmission system in the North of Scotland, was not accepted. This proposal presented an East Coast alternative using existing transmission at cheaper cost and was outlined in skeleton form within his original precognition. A prominent economist had vital evidence expunged from the record. The author also experienced a late submission being rejected. No verbatim record of proceedings was taken for the strategic session of this Inquiry. It was not permissible for the economic case made by Ofgem to be cross-examined within which alternatives had not been explored in their assessment. The investigation of alternative options was not sufficiently rigorous for long distance high voltage direct current (HVDC) options where offsetting compensating benefit did not appear to have been included. A rigid adherence to GB SQSS standards prevented any imaginative proposals becoming explored, especially when the purpose of the proposal was to connect and transmit intermittent wind resource. The consequences arising from limited absorption of intermittent wind resource on the GB Grid system were simply ignored. These failures did not enhance the standing of the Inquiry.

Another consequence with late evidence arose over proposals for HVDC sub-sea cabling to transmit power south to England. These proposals would bypass the major constraint with exporting power from Scotland, across the two border interconnections. Submitted precognition had supported similar alternatives but without detailed and reputable technical analysis could not be sustained. It was only when the strategic session had concluded in May, a report by energy consultancy (TNEI) consultants dated at the end of March came to light giving in-depth analysis of sub-sea cabling around the Scottish coastline and with connections south to Deeside and Wash estuaries. What was so significant with this report was its having been commissioned by Highlands and Islands Enterprise in conjunction with the Scottish Executive and Island Councils. The revelation of such anomalies eventually led to a parliamentary question and debate in the Scottish Parliament being held in September of 2007. In October a submission was forwarded (*Appendix 4C*) to the Scottish Minister for energy making the case for an HVDC connection to bypass the cross border interconnections.

The relevance of these undersea connections came to light in 2009 in transmission connection proposals presented with the Transmission Access Review consultation. Instead of a third cross border high voltage alternating current (HVAC) connection as previously mooted, HVDC sub-sea cables were being proposed to run along both west and east coasts from England, terminating within the central belt and north east Scotland[2].

Objectors were able to reveal a number of flaws with the analysis presented by the applicants. The need for this project to attain the 2020 target for Scottish renewable connection was not established. Once commenced it would become extremely difficult to discontinue the project with completion over a five-year period. When the major constraint lay in exporting power from Scotland across the border interconnection, a strong case could be made for delay, particularly when staged alternatives were available avoiding any environmental footprint and its impact on Scottish tourism. Quite apart from the project being an intrusion in itself, it also enables further desecration across the Grampian Highlands from wind development. The decision to approve the application was described as like taking a razor blade to a Rembrandt.

Considerable commercial benefit lies behind this project, only becoming necessary when government targets post 2020 need to be implemented. It is galling for professional engineering opinion to know such levels cannot be reached without astronomical levels of security investment, if at all. With so much political capital at stake, a rational option for recommending delay with this project was not acceptable.

Notes and Reference

1. The technical report from this Inquiry can be found on
   http://www.scotland.gov.uk/Resource/Doc/917/0088330.pdf
2. DECC ENSG Report 4/3/2009 p65 fig 5.4 – *Our Electricity Network: A Vision for 2020*   http://www.ensg.gov.uk /index.php?article=126

10 Crossing the Divide

*In a democratic society the value of free speech depends on
information being transparent.*

How is the small boy seeing the Emperor pass by able to let the
Emperor know he has a problem? What mechanisms to inform
are available? All too often the individual is constrained by his
employment, the source of his knowledge, where necessary
institutional discipline prevents any public expression of dissent.
What has to be said can be incomprehensible to the public,
inviting apathy, especially from members of the established
media who are notoriously deficient in any technical expertise.
The professional institutions, which often had high standards,
have become marginalised by commercial interests and
increasing amalgamation, no longer sustained by significant
public sector support from nationalised bodies. To illustrate this
concern, the nature of reference from the Institution of
Engineering and Technology (IET) (previously IEE) supporting
Appendix 2 is no longer readily available in that form. Engineers
receive nominal encouragement from the academic
establishment, concentrated among managerial echelons in
symbiotic relationships.

Increasingly, avenues to inform the public through individuals
are derived from retired personnel having a sense of public duty,
who are prepared to take time and trouble in either attending
interminable public inquiries or responding to public consultations.
This approach has many deficiencies as technical information is
no longer provided from utilities and engineers in retirement
become distanced from new innovation. Public inquiries are more

often than not preoccupied with planning law than with technical essentials. Such issues are frequently not adequately understood and, unless of direct relevance to an inquiry, become sidelined, particularly with fragmented wind farm inquiries. Public consultations invariably seek corporate response and, unless submissions are published, give little incentive for individuals to participate. It may come as a surprise to learn the differences of technical opinion that exist within an organisation having common sources of information. Faultlines often emerge between operating branches and head office bureaucratic support departments that can extend to the boardroom where composition of members may not reflect knowledge of the product or services being provided. The suspicion remains that structures within the civil service are similarly infected, raising the question whether such bodies can be fit for purpose.

Even when extending information supply to corporate response, there remains a significant problem with comprehension in the structures of government. One technique to bridge this problem is to commission relevant academic studies that can so easily unravel under practical constraints. Another is to consult with commercial interests that while informed would always seek their own advantage. Smart metering presents a topical example. All too easily commercial advantage may be gained with an issue, as, even though flawed, it would reap benefit to participants if responsibility could be avoided. The trick is not to hold the parcel when the music stops.

Much disquiet surrounds the science of global warming and the interlocking relationships with democratic political control and international negotiation[1]. As if this controversy is not enough with all its related spin and national self-interest, the scale of economic impact with mitigation measures have simply not been addressed in a way to command public confidence. Expectation for the electricity supply industry to bear the brunt of carbon saving measures in the UK is heaping a succession of avoidable costs onto the consumer. These are through a range of charges and subsidies varying from support for renewable technologies (mainly wind), carbon sequestration, electricity grid reinforcement, offshore grids and smart metering. Yet to be introduced are probable subsidies for essential fossil standby generation and nuclear investment. There is money to be made but at whose expense?

Consultations

The Royal Society of Edinburgh in 2006 undertook a comprehensive review of the Scottish energy scene and produced thirty-seven recommendations, including replacing ROC subsidy with a carbon levy, planning guidance and redefining the 2020 target for renewable generation. Evidence was taken from a hundred expert witnesses with almost two hundred written submissions. The report provided one of the most informed documents ever to be written on the subject. In retrospect the document would appear to have been totally ignored by the Scottish administration, in sharp contrast to their own commissioned studies that contained fundamental flaws. (*Appendices 1 and 2*)

The House of Lords have produced a series of reports from Inquiries relating to renewable energy in considerable depth and with extensive informed consultation. One of the most prominent, on *The Economics of Renewable Energy* in 2008, came to a series of significant conclusions:

a) Scepticism that the 2020 renewable targets could be met.
b) The higher costs of raising renewable generation with current policies from 5% to between 30% and 40% would translate into an annual fuel bill increase for the average household of £80.
c) Expectation that intermittent renewable power would result in dependence on electricity supply unprecedented in Europe.
d) Wind generation should be seen largely as additional capacity rather than a substitute for the substantial number of old coal and nuclear plants that are scheduled to be replaced by 2020.

e) The need for a stable investment environment for alternative low carbon power generation.

f) The need to emphasise the development of renewable heat just as much as is being given for renewable generation.

The fourth point above presents by far the most significant challenge. The combination of resources, financial, technical and manufacturing required to construct this scale of generating capacity is immense and would be expected to coincide with considerable capacity in nuclear construction, not due to contribute power until after 2020. In this context the EU renewable commitment for 2020 becomes an irrelevance being a major impediment towards realising essential generation investment over this coming decade. Government response to this report had clearly not grasped the significance of these recommendations.

Some very interesting evidence was submitted from individuals to this Inquiry that would not likely have come from corporate sources. Issues such as: carbon emissions from a national and worldwide perspective; future proposals for interconnection (*Appendix 5A*); the scale of necessary back-up provision; renewable perspective and the cost effectiveness of renewable investment with its accommodation[2]. All these topics went to the heart of the Inquiry illustrating the abundance of information available to those who wished to become informed. In future years when the blame game commences, it can confidently be said the information was available. It is within the structures of government departments and their agencies where failure will be seen to be manifest.

A Department of Business, Enterprise and Regulatory Reform (BERR) Consultation exercise conducted in 2008 gave opportunity for further feedback (*Appendix 5B*). The way this consultation was conducted gave no encouragement for any further contribution. This may in part be explained by the astonishing structural reorganisation from Department of Trade and Industry (DTI) to

BERR then Department of Energy and Climate Change (DECC), all in a matter of months. Once receipt of submission was acknowledged nothing further was heard. It is a source of amazement that the combined functions of energy and climate change can be reconciled within one Department of State when circumscribed by EU treaty obligations of emission reduction, which are widely seen as being unachievable.

Conservative Green Policy Document No 8 provided an opportunity to question official party policy after having been appalled by the lack of technical input within the document (*Appendix 5C*). Given the level of criticism it perhaps came as little surprise to receive no acknowledgement.

National Grid Consultation of July 2009 provided an open statement of anticipated problems arising from increasing intermittence, with suggested solutions. To any informed observer this document was deeply worrying in the scale of innovation being mooted and the rapidly accelerating response required from increasing intermittence. It was clear that some serious technical problems were developing to which they had to respond. The knowledge of National Grid in these matters is unassailable but with responsibility confined to system balancing, as a commercial organisation they had little option but to accept government renewable policy and attempt to make it work. Whatever doubts were held could only be expressed on an informal basis, given the statutory obligation imposed on the civil service to deliver renewable targets. This exercise could be seen as a cry for help or as a warning shot, depending on one's point of view. It cannot be said that information was not made available. The problem rested on the ability for most readers to understand the implications within the document. This is why the spat over smart metering mentioned in Chapter 3 becomes of such significance.

The contribution by the author to this consultation was pointed and direct and not what the recipient would wish to hear (*Appendix 5D*). Again, a delayed acknowledgement was received and nothing further has been heard.

Summary

The whole process of public consultation has serious limitations for any informed specialist who wishes to communicate technical information to the responsible authorities. The examples illustrate the varied difficulties encountered that only serve to discourage any effort being made. It has to be asked why the consultation is being done and with what interest in mind. Does the conduct of the consultation exercise achieve an acceptable standard? Does the recipient have sufficient technical knowledge to ask the right questions or to understand what is being said? All indications suggest paralysis exists on technical issues within the structures of government departments and their agencies where comprehension is seen as being absent.

References
1. http://www.publicservice.co.uk/feature_story.asp?id=13015
2. House of Lords Inquiry – *The Economics of Renewable Energy* – Nov 2008. Evidence pages 335,231,306,480 and 405.

11 Why Does Electricity Cost So Much?

*In the final analysis it is not so much the provision of energy
that matters but its cost.*

It is time to bring together the various conditions mentioned in
previous chapters forming the economic environment to determine
a price the customer must pay for his electricity. By now it should
be clear just how much depends upon decisions taken over many
decades that were essentially technical in character with long-term
perspective in mind. Structures were resilient to political
interference, providing longer-term vision for planning and
research facilities. National need had fuel self-sufficiency as a
priority. All this changed with the 1990 privatisation of the
electrical supply industry when an open market was created that
soon had to be adjusted to accommodate complications arising
from the nuclear generation portfolio.

The new structures created became a home for the
accountants. Asset sweating and equity finance in a fragmented
market had to accommodate increasing regulation imposed by
politicians with growing concern over environmental issues. This
regulation became EU inspired. In a remarkably short period we
have become import dependent with our fuel supplies for electricity
generation and the indigenous manufacturing base that sustained
previous generation investment is no longer available.

Ageing plant has become an issue of real concern. Combined
with Large Combustion Plant Directive (LCPD) regulation, over
this coming decade, substantial coal and nuclear capacity is to be
withdrawn making electricity supply increasingly dependent upon
gas supplies. The attempt to diversify into uneconomic renewable

generation, particularly wind, is inflicting such economic damage and investment paralysis that it has become self-defeating in its aim of import substitution. What has not been sufficiently recognised are the economic penalties that accompany methods to accommodate intermittence: standby plant, interconnection and demand management. Without such expensive measures, supply would be at increasing risk of disconnection and voltage reduction. The lights going out are of concern but so is the knowledge that money will be thrown at the problem in attempts to prevent this from happening.

Policy direction has much to answer for in creating this entirely avoidable scenario. Against Ofgem advice[1] the Renewable Obligation has not only been maintained but extended, then made selective[2]. Further imposition on the electricity consumer comes from support for Carbon Capture and Storage (CCS) development[3] and 'smart' metering[4] in addition to the extensive costs for Grid connection and reinforcement, operational accommodation and premature connection for intermittent wind resource[5]. The sums involved are mind-bending and though Ofgem has a nominal responsibility to scrutinise expenditure, with Ministerial ambition towards renewable targets, financial discipline becomes relegated to a very low priority. A reading of the 2005 'Freds' report, 'realising the 2020 target' produced by the Scottish Executive provides ample evidence for spending largesse[6] where renewable energy is a partial devolved responsibility. What cannot be ignored is the developing public mood as revealed by reactions to events such as the Met Office predictions, Climatic Research Unit (CRU) scandal, the collapse of Copenhagen with UN Intergovernmental Panel on Climate Change (IPCC) credibility and harsh winters. When awareness of financial interest is added from carbon trading, leading to strategic closure of Redcar steelmaking, rising fuel bills through subsidy and parliamentary expense scandals, no politician should underestimate the electoral reaction.

It cannot have escaped the notice of most consumers how tariffs have markedly increased over these last few years and stayed high despite the ramping down of gas prices that prompted the initial surge. Since privatisation, gas has become a dominant component of the generation mix whose cost is highly sensitive to fuel prices. A plethora of energy regulation schemes have arisen with associated trading where costs can only ultimately be borne by the end user whose fuel options have become increasingly limited when tied to gas supply.

The electricity consumer is captive to all these Government inspired measures where any options are confined within EU directives. What is certain is that none of the fragmented utilities will become disadvantaged by this circumstance and will seek to buttress their position for the inevitable scale of generation and transmission investment required following so many years of neglect. As matters stand the consumer can expect no relief with their electricity bills, indeed they are set to continue rising to unsustainable levels. Only change of government policy can bring relief and given the similar approach to energy policy taken by all three main political parties, the prospect of change is not promising.

Something will have to be done to alleviate the position of the energy poor, a scandal that the media seem to have overlooked. The suggestion of demand management disconnection with reduced tariff may have an appeal but what is unsustainable are the generous subsidies to be given for micro-generation supply due to come into effect from April 2010[7]. This policy measure, common to both main parties, is socially selective and effectively denies participation for those living in high-density locations. This measure only perpetuates an uneconomic energy strategy that inevitably will become subsidised by the long-suffering electricity consumer.

Notes and References
1. *Reform of the Renewables Obligation 2006: Ofgem's response.* Ref 11/07 January 2007.
2. ReNews 17/12/2009 Issue 182 page 11.

3. Telegraph website 25 Nov 2009. E-ON *chief fears clean coal may never be viable.*
   http://www.telegraph.co.uk/finance/newsbysector/energy/6655585/
   E.ON-chief-Paul-Golby-fears-clean-coal-may-never-be-viable.html

4. Times Online 3 Dec 2009. *National Grid fears 'smart metering' being rushed.*
   http://business.timesonline.co.uk/tol/business/industry_sectors/
   natural_resources/article6941944.ece

5. Ofgem press release R/21 of 8/5/2009 – *Connection of 450MW low carbon generation.*

6. *Scotland's Renewable Energy Potential: realising the 2020 target.* Scottish Executive – June 2005.

7. Times Online 12 July 2009. *Cheap 'green mortgages' to foster energy-saving homes.*
   http://www.timesonline.co.uk/tol/news/environment/article6689632.
   ece

12 The Way Forward?

It may be a weed instead of a fish that, after all my labour, I may at last pull up.

Michael Faraday

The nominal justification for renewable resource development has been climate change mitigation. The science used to justify this need for carbon dioxide (CO_2) reduction has become increasingly questioned. Government has an interest by being able to introduce policy whose costs can be passed directly on to the general public as consumers without parliamentary scrutiny. Vast sums of money become involved with carbon trading. Whole industries are dependent upon renewable subsidies with a pervasive influence across many professions. The role of the UN Intergovernmental Panel on Climate Change (IPCC) agency is becoming discredited. The vested interests affected are indeed powerful so it can be expected rational change will not come overnight.

Incentive for the developer is only one component of many varied and opaque charges that are being passed onto the electricity consumer. Preoccupation over EU renewable targets, combined with the issues surrounding subsidies, has created extensive uncertainty over essential investment into conventional coal and nuclear generation, forcing even greater dependence upon gas supplies. The scale of retirement of nuclear and coal generation over this coming decade through age and environmental regulation presents a series of challenges whose urgency to resolve is on a parallel with that of the banking crisis. The cost of measures to overcome intermittence from renewable energy are set to rocket. The investment needed to replace the existing generation portfolio is on a scale that would equal the highest historical rates that were necessary forty years ago without the manufacturing base and skilled workforce that then existed.

Current policy to promote extensive scale of wind resource is thoroughly misconceived. The stability risk is considered quite unacceptable. Comparable standby generation capacity would require to be available whose fluctuating response would reduce its operational life. The necessary scale of transmission connection and reinforcement bears cost comparison with the associated wind farm development. The burden having to be borne by the electricity consumer can only promote extensive fuel poverty. The legacy for posterity is landscape despoliation onshore and future navigational hazards offshore on an extensive scale. Promotion for jobs and energy supply is illusory as manufacturing capacity is based overseas and energy provision ruinously expensive when compared to alternative options.

Technically the support for uneconomic intermittent renewable generation cannot continue without serious risk of grid instability, only delayed by the need for mitigating measures at unsustainable cost. Indeed cost in itself would be justification enough to terminate support. The very existence of renewable subsidy in all its forms should be discontinued as this interventionist approach presents uncertainty to the private developer, preventing investment into nuclear and coal technologies so desperately needed to restore a sound generation mix. In relying upon gas, the nation becomes hostage to fortune to such a degree as to invite further impoverishment for its citizens. A decision has to be made to either pursue carbon mitigation with generation supply or invest for power supply security; it is simply not possible to have both given the resources and timescale available.

There is concern with the scale of ageing plant leading to unreliability and closure, the very necessary nuclear programme that has at least a decade to run before power starts to become available and the strategic need to avoid further gas dependence; all this circumstance comes together to give only one logical option to cover power supply shortages in the available timescale. Coal generation has to be reinstated without regulatory constraint, both to permit new more efficient investment and to allow existing generation capacity to continue operating until sufficient nuclear capacity comes on stream. The decision by subsidiary of E.ON Netz (formerly PowerGen) (E.ON UK) to postpone the supercritical coal-fired power station at Kingsnorth is the very opposite of what is necessary and without such investment, electricity prices will rise even further[1]. If carbon capture and storage (CCS) technology is required, it should become the responsibility of the State to provide. Large Combustion Plant Directive (LCPD) and Industrial Emissions Directive (IED) regulation has to be rescinded[2] with 12GW of coal-fired capacity expected to retire by 2015.

The increasing problem of grid system balancing to cater for intermittence is seen to be the critical technical issue accommodating further renewable resource. A more engineering orientated solution is needed away from the pervasive market approach of contracts with adjustment by price signals. The merit order method of generation scheduling under nationalisation experienced by the author was considered as being far superior than the subsequent straitjacketed procedures endured with costed contract arrangements made since privatisation. While trading contracts are necessary between operating systems, the extent of detail into generation supply becomes an impediment and could be avoided by a more generalised contract condition based upon duration of generator operation. The point to be made is that authority for generation scheduling and system balancing should be handled by engineers, not traders.

A year long study by Ofgem has recognised that existing structures cannot continue to manage the range of problems arising within the UK for electrical power supply[3]. Current arrangements have no defined overall technical responsibility, restricting any scope for initiative. The document has to accommodate government policy for renewable development on one hand with impending realities of ageing plant, regulation and gas import dependency on the other, all when financial conditions have deteriorated. But can state intervention deliver when the existing situation has been largely induced by the State itself? Engineering capability is very much concentrated with overseas concerns for both supply and organisation. Whatever structure is eventually adopted, only the State can resolve regulation issues and renewable target commitments. Without necessary confidence, no system can provide results.

There is an alternative option to consider. Development of a tidal barrage on the Severn Estuary would provide reliable and predictable power without the scale of transmission loss that would result from renewable resource exploitation from Scotland. Major operational benefit would be given if this energy output could be dovetailed with other barrages or tidal flow technologies around the coastline to present an aim towards consistent power output over the daily cycle and so avoid power supply fluctuations based upon the lunar day. The structure of organisation to institute this programme, envisaged as a State agency independent of the Treasury and answerable directly to Parliament, would provide necessary control facilities that could centralise all other renewable generation. Such change would present an opportunity to reform and regularise the highly dubious and unsustainable current financial arrangements for subsidy. This organisation could also provide the facility for longer term strategic planning and have the necessary commercial and industrial backbone, free from political vicissitudes that have so enfeebled the long-term direction of national energy policy. This organisation would bring together other promising renewable technologies such as remaining hydro resource, into a more coherent structure that would consider all factors towards development options. Management of funding grants across the spectrum of renewable research and development would have more focussed application than through government departments.

Over the longer term, increasing nuclear development would constrain fossil expansion, particularly if technical advance could enable more flexibility such as the ability to shut down overnight. This feature of the nuclear fast breeder reactor (FBR) technology would make profitable use of spent fuel in storage and 'close' the nuclear fuel cycle[4]. Increasing scale of nuclear development would pressure more economic use of nuclear fuel where existing facility in this country has an international standing. Above all, certainty with lower electricity pricing would create sustainable growth and an aim towards strategic energy independence, avoiding foreign entanglements.

Such strategy avoids fully enmeshing the GB Grid system into the European controlled system. The potential of the nuclear reprocessing industry would be enhanced, becoming an international supplier of nuclear fuel, enabling leverage over the issue of nuclear proliferation. Expertise with renewable development would continue as a future insurance and some discipline introduced into the distortions arising from private initiative. Most of all, a long-term view would be established where subsidy and grants would have proper control. A body of expertise would be available to advise government policy and be in a position to contain the debris from this ill-advised adventure into wind resource.

Problems are an opportunity. Given vision and commitment, an alternative plan has to be available for the time when politicians realise the present course cannot be sustained.

References

1. Trade journal *Building* 8 Oct 2009. *E-ON puts £1.5 billion Kingsnorth power station on hold.*
   http://www.building.co.uk/story.asp?storycode=3150487&origin=bldgdailynewsletter
2. The *Guardian*. 18 January 2010. *E-ON chief – Preserve coal plants to keep lights on.* http://www.guardian.co.uk/business/2010/jan/18/eon-coal-plant-plea
3. Ofgem Consulation Document 3 Feb 2010. Ref 16/10. *Project Discovery – Options for delivering secure and sustainable energy supplies.* http://www.ofgem.gov.uk/MARKETS/WHLMKTS/DISCOVERY/Documents1/Project_Discovery_ FebConDoc_FINAL.pdf
4. *The Economist Technology Quarterly* 12 Dec 2009 page 17

13 Epilogue

'But facts are chiels that winna ding, An' downa be disputed,'
Robert Burns

The design of any ship has to compromise a range of requirements: seakeeping, stability, function and suitability for its sphere of operations. Supporting facilities for logistical support and maintenance must also be available. With the existing state of electricity supply we have a situation where the ship is old, its trade routes restricted, shore based facilities sold off and the engine hammered by constant speed changing. The design is no longer suitable for what the owner has in mind and he wants to revert to sail as he considers the engine fumes would upset the passengers. Unfortunately, he has no business sense but is wily enough to con the passengers for extra cash, convincing them the fumes would be lethal. Meanwhile the ship is about to face a gathering storm. It does not help with the skipper having been paid off but the multinational crew are biding their time knowing they are well paid and stand to make a killing once the sails are seen to be inadequate. As for the passengers, they are stuck on a boat and have to experience the storm before realising their error, knowing they can do nothing until they get ashore and lobby for a new owner.

Once the passengers are ashore it is only the start of their problems. They would find the owner is really only a steward and it is they who have to face the eye-watering bills that must be paid, stretching on for a quarter of a century. Experience has shown becalming to be unacceptable so an engine is needed after all. They would also find the purchased sails were bought on a false prospectus and the preoccupation with fitting them came with neglect for the engine. There was even the opportunity for an engine refit but the owner was persuaded that sails looked so much nicer and he could make money by selling off some onshore facilities. Unfortunately, most had already withered away because they had never been used.

So how are the passengers to go about finding a replacement engine? Well the neighbouring ports are rubbing their hands with glee, knowing they have a soft market that will pay up as the engine is on its last legs. If the trade routes are kept frozen then they can force a bargain. They also know the ship has to be modified to take their larger off-the-shelf product, realising the modifications already carried out for fitting the sails have been next to useless and worse, compromised the ship's stability. Not only that, a temporary engine has to be fitted where the fuel suppliers are not always on the best of terms with the customer and the neighbours know few others can supply that particular engine, at least with the quantities needed as indigenous supplies are rapidly becoming exhausted.

By now the passengers are getting a bit fed up as the bills keep pouring in and some of them just cannot afford to keep on paying. They have had to fork out for all sorts of expensive fancy gadgets that never worked and they are not convinced the new steward will be up to the job. They need to know they can choose the right engine without strings attached and that trade routes can be unfrozen to give them time to get it right. They have been appalled to find out the previous steward had not even bothered to seek technical advice before fitting any of the sails, as he would not be held directly to account for the bills. The situation is even worse as his predecessor had sacked the naval architect that could have warned him off all the future mad cap schemes dreamt up by chums within the owners club which had been infiltrated by all sorts of carpet baggers.

The realisation has slowly dawned on the passengers of the consequences that come from not having nor even listening to the professionals. They now recognise an imperative for a trusted cadre of principled, qualified and experienced support, needing to be impartial and worldly-wise, to be made responsible and left to get on with what needs doing without interference. The task to restore the ship to a proper condition will take decades. It will be seen by the impoverished passengers as a necessary pill to swallow after all their bitter experience. The final irony of this disaster is that in large measure it could so easily have been avoided had the owner listened to a master mariner before they set sail.

Glossary of Abbreviations

AC – alternating current

AGR – advanced gas-cooled reactor

ASA – Advertising Standards Authority

BERR – Department of Business, Enterprise and Regulatory Reform (*formerly* DTI)

BETTA – British Electricity Trading and Transmission Arrangements

BDLG – Beauly Denny Landscape Group

CCGT – combined cycle gas turbine

CCS – carbon capture and storage

CEGB – Central Electricity Generating Board

CHP – combined heat and power

CLOWD – Campaign to Limit Onshore Windfarm Development

CO_2 – carbon dioxide

CRU – Climatic Research Unit

CV – calorific value

DC – direct current

DECC – Department of Energy and Climate Change (formerly BERR)

DNOs – distribution network operators

DSOs – distribution system operators

DTI – Department of Trade and Industry

DUKES – Digest of UK Energy Statistics

ENSG – Electricity Networks Strategy Group

E.ON. UK – subsidiary of E.ON Netz (formerly PowerGen)

E.ON. Netz – German based power company

EU – European Union

FBR – fast breeder reactor

GB SQSS – Great Britain Security and Quality of Supply Standards

GW – gigawatts (1,000MW)

GWh – gigawatt-hours

HIE – Highlands and Islands Enterprise

HVAC – high voltage alternating current

HVDC – high voltage direct current

IEC – International Electrotechnical Commission

IED – Industrial Emissions Directive

IEE – Institution of Electrical Engineers (now IET)

IET – Institution of Engineering and Technology

IEV – International Electrotechnical Vocabulary

IPC – Infrastructure Planning Commission

IPCC – UN Intergovernmental Panel on Climate Change

kV – kilovolts

kW – kilowatt (1,000 watts)

kWh – kilowatt-hours

LCPD – Large Combustion Plant Directive

MW – megawatts (1,000 kW)

MWh – megawatt-hours

NETA – New Electricity Trading Arrangements

NGET – National Grid Electrical Transmission Ltd

NGT – National Grid Transco

MVA – mega volt ampere (1,000 kVA)

OCGT – open circuit gas turbine

Ofgem – Office of Gas and Electricity Markets (energy regulator)

RO – Renewables Obligation

ROC – Renewables Obligation Certificate

RSE – Royal Society of Edinburgh

SCADA – system control, alarms and data acquisition

SHETL – Scottish Hydro Electric Transmission Ltd

SSE – Scottish and Southern Energy plc

SP – Scottish Power plc

SPTL – Scottish Power Transmission Ltd

SYS – Seven Year Statements

TNEI – (Energy Consultancy)

TNPG – The Nuclear Power Group (nuclear consortia)

TSOs – transmission system operators

TWh – terrawatt-hours

UCTE – Union for the Co-ordination of Transmission of Electricity

UKERC – United Kingdom Energy Research Centre

Appendix 1

Issues for Scotland's Energy Supply: Submission by Alan Shaw to the Royal Society of Edinburgh

"Kelvin to Weir, and on to GB SYS 2005"

1. Introduction

Born, educated and initially trained as a professional engineer in Edinburgh I am delighted to contribute to the above Inquiry. I will limit my submission to aspects, including those in Scotland, of GB Supergrid 2005, and of renewable energy and nuclear power.

I am glad that RSE has restricted contributions to organisations and individuals with relevant experience. The growing governmental tendency to set up open public consultations on such complex matters tends to muddy the waters and delay decision making.

Timely is the comment by Professor Maxwell Irvine that "energy is an emotive subject and too important to become a party political issue". It is a matter of concern among chartered engineers, at all levels, that in the UK it has become so, and too often debated by individuals, including government ministers, manifestly with no technical knowledge of the subject whatsoever and disinclined to take professional advice.

I have read the consultation questions with a sense of *deja vu*. Fifty years ago I was invited to join one of the industrial consortia set up to implement urgently the UK White Paper Programme of Atomic Energy. In addition to our enjoyably strenuous "day jobs" midnight oil had often to be burned to submit collective thoughts to the broadsheet press and technical journals about the future of nuclear versus other forms of power generation.

Our mother company owned a leading fundamental research laboratory studying fusion power. In those far off days the time scale for economic take off of fusion power seemed to be about thirty years. Nothing has changed – it is still thirty years! But the problem is akin to putting a piece of the sun safely into an invisible magnetic bottle and safely making a reliable profit out of it for a further thirty years. That does not come cheaply – or quickly.

For the RSE Inquiry the most valuable predictions and advice will obviously come from bodies and individuals with long term financial, commercial and operational interests in energy matters. Fifteen years, rather than fortyfive, seem to me a more credible range for projections.

Leading sources of information in the electricity field are the three transmission companies, National Grid plc, Scottish Power plc and Scottish and Southern Energy plc/ Scottish Hydro plc.

Under the terms of their transmission licences they have each for several years produced a rolling annual Seven Year Statement of their plans and operations. From 1 April 2005 this task has become unified by the appointment of National Grid plc as GB System Operator and producer, with the collaboration of the two Scottish companies, of the new GB Seven Year Statement, GB SYS 2005.

Already seamlessly on the Internet, this is a dynamic textbook of the planning and operation of one of the largest and most compact electricity systems in the world, to which Scotland has greatly contributed from the very beginning of the national grid.

The Great Britain basis has apparently arisen because the UK public electric supply industry is under two separate Regulators-OFGEM for mainland Great Britain and OFREG for Northern Ireland. The Northern Ireland electricity system is almost identical in annual maximum demand (c.1600MW) to that of Scottish Hydro plc. Although it also is a 50 cycle AC system it is not synchronised with the GB system because the 500MW Scotland – Northern Ireland Moyle submarine Interconnector is HV DC.

The National Grid plc submission to this RSE Inquiry is limited to one page. But that page points to three documents which

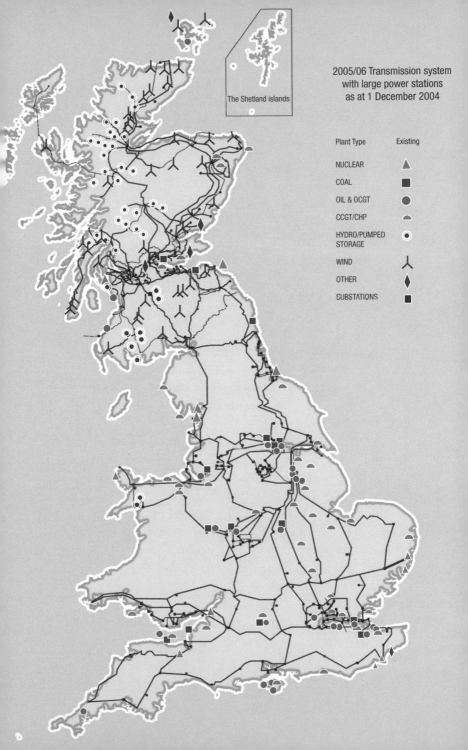

2005/06 Transmission system
with large power stations
as at 1 December 2004

The Shetland islands

Plant Type	Existing
NUCLEAR	▲
COAL	■
OIL & OCGT	●
CCGT/CHP	◗
HYDRO/PUMPED STORAGE	⊙
WIND	⅄
OTHER	◆
SUBSTATIONS	■

are required reading for such an Inquiry. They are the Ten Year Statement (TYS) in gas, the Seven Year Statement (SYS) in electricity, and a paper "Transporting Britain's energy" (gas to 2014/15).

For those interested in the evolution of the UK grid system I offer a few historical notes. Engineering is the application of science to human need. Much political lip service is paid to reduction of costs and the increase of efficiency. The national grid was formed to make those objectives continuously attainable in the fields of generation, transmission and distribution.

2. Public lighting by electricity

The initial public interest in electricity in the nineteenth century focussed on the possibility of lighting superior to the whale oil lamp or the flaring "fishtail" gas burner.

From 1856 for about thirty years four UK lighthouses in south east England were illuminated experimentally by Professor F H Holmes's invention of carbon-arc lamps powered by primitive steam driven alternators. For domestic use the intense light of carbon arc electrodes was too brilliant and too costly for domestic use. Increased safety at sea justified the high cost. There the brilliance was welcomed.

In 1876 P. Jablochkoff, a Russian officer working in Paris, invented his famous "electric candle" – the first carbon arc lamp cheap enough to be used on a large scale and using AC for equal consumption of the two carbon rods. Experimental public lighting installations appeared in both Paris and London in 1877. Large football matches were occasionally played under this brilliant glare. 1880 saw Sir Joseph Swan's residence in Low Fell, Gateshead as the first house in Britain, possibly in the world, to be lit by incandescent electric bulbs, giving the softer illumination and lower cost required.

In 1884 Dr John Hopkinson of London showed mathematically that, contrary to general opinion, alternators could be run connected in parallel. This set the scene worldwide for the centralising of alternators in power stations.

3. The steam turbine and economies of scale

The same year, 1884, brought the filing of two patents on the steam turbine and the commissioning in the same year of the world's first turbo-generating set (of 7.5kW/DC) all by the Hon Charles Parsons of Newcastle-upon-Tyne.

Until then electricity generators had been driven by large and noisy reciprocating steam engines, they could not run on superheated steam without costly cylinder lubrication systems.

The steam turbine ran quietly and without vibration. Most importantly, it offered, with advances in metallurgy over time, huge economies of scale, with substantial reductions in capital cost per Megawatt (MW) for each doubling of designed MW capacity. The reciprocating engine was now obsolete and individual turbine-alternator sets increased in designed output from 1MW in 1900 to the world's largest (Germany) of 1,300 MW by 1976. The size of the electricity network places an upper limit on the largest turbo-alternator which can be installed. In the UK the largest standard sets are each 660 MW gross output.

4. Thermodynamic efficiency (including notes on CHP)

For thermal plant, overall thermal efficiency is governed by a law of thermodynamics stating that the higher the turbine inlet steam temperature and pressure and lower the exhaust steam temperature and pressure the higher the overall thermal efficiency.

Steadily improving metallurgy has allowed thermal efficiency of power station generation gradually to be increased, from around 22 per cent in 1939 to about 42 per cent. With such improvements made possible by increased steam pressures and temperatures the inlet steam pipes of large modern turbines glow cherry red, but invisibly under thermal lagging and planished steel outer casings.

In recent years UK political interest in efficiency of electricity generation has focussed on "Combined Heat and Power" (CHP) in the belief that this is a high efficiency (80 per cent) way of generating electricity. It is an already well known extension of the law of thermodynamics mentioned above. But it is an application peculiar to the economic production of low pressure, low temperature steam as a process heat source in many and various manufacturing processes.

To raise large quantities of steam of such low thermodynamic quality with a dedicated steam boiler and pass it straight to the process would be very expensive indeed. This cost is enormously reduced by raising steam at power station levels of pressure and temperature, passing it through a steam turbine driving an alternator and exhausting the steam directly to the process at the pressure and temperature required.

Under this system the combined energy produced as electricity and as heat in process steam is as much as 80 per cent of the energy in the steam raising boiler fuel. The point apparently missed by government in setting an annual CHP target far above the original national level is that the electricity produced is a by-product totally subservient in rate of production to the varying process heat rate required. The market in which to sell the idea of CHP is therefore only of financial interest to large process heat users able to sell-on any surplus electricity produced.

If, as may often be the case, the variations in process steam demand and therefore byproduct electricity produced, do not match the daily pattern of demand by the grid locally then surplus electricity can become a liability not an asset, as there is normally no means of storing it.

DTI July 2005 annual figures show that, in the four years commencing 2000, CHP installed capacity (expressed as MWe = megawatts electric = maximum continuous rating of the alternator, not electricity produced in the year) were at a uniform level of about 4,750 MWe. In 2004 the level rose to about 5,300 MW/e. The government target is still 10,000 MWe.

5. AC or DC? – The "battle of the systems"

From 1886 to 1900 there was a "battle of the systems" with Lord Kelvin, Thomas Edison and others fighting a rearguard action on behalf of direct current (DC) against progressives such as Sebastian

V.Z. de Ferranti and George Westinghouse, promoting alternating current (AC). This offered cheap voltage transformation for reduction of transmission line losses and the universal use of cheap, simple and reliable asynchronous induction motors.

In USA this competition was red in tooth and claw. Edison designed the world's first electric chair for the execution of criminals and sold it to the prison authorities specifying that it should be operated using "Westinghouse current" i.e. AC, promoted by his rival!

In 1887 a French metal syndicate cornered much of the world's copper supplies, forcing up prices and highlighting the main advantage of A.C – cheap voltage transformation. (Today power electronics allow DC to compete with AC in this feature on high voltage power lines.)

6. Thermal losses in electrical conductors

In an electrical circuit power in watts equals volts times amperes. Thermal losses in conductors equal the square of the current in amperes, times volts. Therefore transmission losses can be reduced by raising voltage, thereby minimising current for a given power.

The optimum voltage is decided by balancing savings due to thermal loss reduction against increase in capital cost of insulation of conductors e.g. longer insulator strings and taller towers.

Underground high voltage transmission cables can be twenty times as costly as overhead lines and maintenance more difficult and time consuming.

7. Tesla's polyphase electricity system

By 1900 the UK electricity supply industry had taken off economically. That year saw the first public supply of three phase current (from the new Neptune Bank power station, Tyneside, designed by Charles Merz).

This system was invented by the Serbian Nikola Tesla who emigrated to America to work for George Westinghouse. In it, the stator of an alternator is wound with the equivalent of three separate alternators in one machine but physically separated at an angle of 120 degrees to each other. One end of each of the three windings is bonded to the other two to form an earthed "star point".

Vectorial mathematics show that the combined alternator output now requires, not six power lines but only three, accompanied by a small wire to take out of balance currents and to run along the top of transmission towers for earthing and lightning protection. Thus the Tesla three phase system economises enormously in copper, and throughout the entire electricity system.

8. Statement by Lord Kelvin of Largs

In his inaugural address at the official opening of Neptune Bank in 1901 the great scientist/ engineer of the nineteenth century, Lord Kelvin of Largs (William Thomson), famously said: "I don't know what electricity is, and cannot define it – I have spent my life on it. I do not know the limit of electricity, but it will go beyond the limit of anything we conceive of today."

This charmingly frank Scottish polymath had, en passant, by inventing and patenting a wide range of electrical equipment, by being a consultant on the transatlantic cable and a partner in two engineering consulting firms, become a wealthy man who could afford a 126 foot yacht ("Lalla Rookh") and a baronial estate. His advice was valued in gold.

He had also dominated by the sheer power of his intellect the fields not only of electricity and magnetism but also of thermodynamics, hydrodynamics, geophysics, tides, the shape of the earth, its rotation and geomagnetism. He also opposed Charles Darwin's theory of evolution, remaining "on the side of the angels". He died in 1907 and was buried in Westminster Abbey.

9. Enter, the 132kV grid

Meanwhile the UK electricity supply industry continued to develop, as disparate municipal electricity undertakings and a few large private companies. *There was no coordinating body* and little or no electrical interconnection. Some were on DC, some on AC and the latter ran on various frequencies from a flickering 25 cycles per second to cycles.

By 1925, the government had become alarmed by the chaotic existence of this huge electrical ragbag of private enterprise based on 500 mainly municipal power stations, tiny by today's standards and including 80 per cent spare capacity for security of supply.

Fortunately, possibly mindful of Kelvin's statement, Stanley Baldwin's administration delegated the solution to a dynamic Glasgow engineering industrialist, Lord Weir. He, with leading consulting engineers such as Charles Merz, quickly drew up a recommended framework for the whole UK electricity supply industry.

The Electricity (Supply) Act 1926 embodied into law the Weir Committee's proposals, establishing the Central Electricity Board which was empowered to design and construct a 132kV national grid and force the replacement of all existing stations as fast as a few very large, thermally efficient "selected" power stations could be built to take their place.

Implementation took place with astonishing speed. The first grid tower in the UK was erected in 1928 near Edinburgh. The first of the large "selected" stations was Portobello, Edinburgh, from which on 30 April 1930 the first section of the new 132 kV UK national grid, the Central Scotland Electricity Scheme, was switched on by Herbert Morrison, the Minister of Transport.

The UK grid was largely completed by 1935, reducing by 1938 the proportion of spare plant necessary from the former 80 per cent to about 15 per cent. The resulting capital saving amounted to 75 per cent of the cost of building the grid and generating costs fell by 24 per cent.

10. Putting the "national" into "grid"!

The 132 kV grid was originally intended to be operated as a number of normally independent regional grids. Each could be connected to a neighbouring regional grid if and when required. The approach of World War required the setting up, in London, of a bomb-proof national grid control centre. With some trepidation the inter-regional isolating switches were closed and as nothing untoward happened they were never reopened except in emergency. The grid was truly national from there on and made an enormous contribution to the war effort.

The nationwide interconnection of the grid forced upon the Central Electricity Board by war emergency conditions introduced the possibility of long distance bulk transmission. This became increasingly valuable in the immediate postwar period when rising electricity demands raced new power station construction.

11. How the grid improved power station economics

The UK was still almost entirely coal based, and in 2004 were still using 50 million tons of coal per annum. From north to south were groups of coalfields, the Scottish Central Belt, Northumberland-Durham with the Cumberland field to the west, a hugegroup in the Midlands, then the South Wales- Forest of Dean- Bristol group and in the distant south east, the small Kent coalfield.

By about 1960 nearly all coal was machine mined and 70 per cent of production was of "smalls" – unsuitable for domestic and many other uses. It was virtually a byproduct of machine mining and ideal for large power stations with coal mills reducing it to a fine dust and blowing it into cathedrals of flame.

This was the cheapest of coals and its cost ranged from between £5 and £6 per ton in the older coalfields to as little as £3.50 on the East Midlands coalfield. The cost of electricity sent out from the new super power stations was typically 0.5p per kWh, made up as to annual capital charges (of £50 per kW) 0.10p, operation and maintenance 0.05p and coal price (at £3.50 per ton) 0.35p.

To transport coal by rail in the UK then cost £1 per ton per 100 miles = 0.10p per kWh for a base load station. The grid could carry all the coal required as electricity at a fraction of the rail transportation costs. The oil equivalent of small coal was residual fuel oil after the refinery had distilled around a thousand more volatile products from the imported crude petroleum. The grid enabled power stations to be built near refineries (e.g. Stanlow and Fawley) and the residual fuel oil converted into electricity at the cheapest price and transported away to distant centres of demand cheaply by the grid.

12. The grid and hydro-electric power

Hydro-electric power, which in the UK is already virtually fully developed, is generated in the mountainous regions of the country; in northern Scotland (the former North of Scotland Hydro-Electric Board), in the Clyde valley, in south western Scotland (Galloway) and also in Wales. The national grid is connected to them all and takes away, as required, to centres of demand all over the UK the output of these beautiful parts of the UK. The centre of gravity of UK electricity demand is well south of a line drawn from the Bristol Channel to the Wash. There is therefore a steady flow of electricity from Scotland and northern England to the south.

The grid is also similarly connected to large pumped storage stations (Cruachan 400MW, and Foyers 300MW) in the Highlands of Scotland and Dinorwig (1,728 MW) and Ffestiniog, (360 MW) in North Wales. These, using night time off peak electricity from adjacent (in grid terms) base load nuclear power stations to pump water uphill, meet the daily peak loads of the main centres of population in central Scotland and the Liverpool region respectively by letting down water as hydro-electric power during such times

None of these pumped storage stations are generating "primary" electricity from rainfall. They are extraordinarily useful devices for lopping day time peaks off regional demands. One of the reasons they are so useful both for this and for meeting unexpected voids in intermittent production from e.g. wind turbines, is the unique ability of hydro turbines to pick up full load from standstill, in a minute or so. However, nothing in engineering is free! About one quarter of the kWh generated is used to pump the water uphill again. But it is a much valued operational facility and has pulled the grid out of overload situations many times.

13. The grid and nuclear power

When, in February 1955, the government published its White Paper "A programme for nuclear power", the existence of the UK national grid made it easy to site the new commercial nuclear electricity stations in remote locations.

Their turbines receive non-radioactive steam from the nuclear reactor heat exchangers and exhaust it, as from fossil fuelled power stations, into condensers. The steam, condensed on the outer surfaces of sea water cooled metal tubes, gravitates into the condenser sump and is immediately pumped back into the nuclear heat exchangers as boiler feedwater in a completely closed cycle.

The North Wales 400 kV grid has an interesting configuration embracing in its ring a number of natural flow and pumped storage hydro stations with a spur line to Anglesey's Wylfa (1,081MW) nuclear power station, thus minimising the transmission line losses when using nuclear base load generation to pump water up to the high level reservoirs of Dinorwig (1,728 MW) and Ffestiniog (360 MW). Another spur connects the ring to the Liverpool and West Midlands regions of the grid for peak lopping.

The Supergrid grid connects installations as far apart as the Dounreay nuclear site on the north coast of Scotland and the two Dungeness nuclear power stations on the English Channel coast 530 miles south, as well as Hunterson B and Torness in the Scottish central belt and the other nuclear power stations south of the Border.

Nuclear power stations as compared to coal and oil fired power stations are characteristically of high capital cost per kilowatt but low running cost per kilowatt hour. For optimum overall system economy they are run continuously at as near full load as possible, normally only being withdrawn for routine annual maintenance, as for other types of plant. The system base load is their natural habitat.

It is therefore costly to run them as standby for any form of unpredictable intermittent energy connected to the system. Also due to their massive construction their response time to outages of volatile intermittent plant are too slow. They can however be used to cover slower variations in system load.

In France, in the nationalised Electricité de France grid, because of absence of indigenous fuel resources, over 75 per cent of the total electricity demand in MWh is met by 58 pressurised water reactors similar to but not identical to our Sizewell B power station in Suffolk. Their combined capacity of over 62,000 MWe is equivalent to the present GB annual maximum instantaneous demand.

14. Commercial secrecy

In Section 9 above ("Enter, the 132 kV Grid") Portobello power station, Edinburgh, was mentioned as being the first "selected" station connected to the UK grid under the 1926 Electricity (Supply Act. It had been formally opened by King George V in 1923. The third and final stage, bringing its output up to just over 146MW, was opened in the summer of 1939 by the Rt Hon Sir Thomas Mackay Cooper MP, Lord Advocate of Scotland.

An interesting feature of the Portobello 1939 Commemorative Brochure is that it lists in great detail the capital costs, the generation costs for 1937-38 and the electricity output figures for 1937 and 1938. Such figures are difficult if not impossible to obtain for new stations today. Yet in other countries it has been possible for visiting foreign engineers to have frank discussions with power companies about project and other costs. Few or no inhibitions about exchanging such figures have been encountered. The UK appears still to have a reputation for secrecy in discussion of costs and "commercially sensitive" information.

In 1949 a delegation from the British Electricity Authority (predecessor of the CEGB) sent a delegation to the United States and Canada led by Sir John Hacking. It reported in particular on the latest practices adopted by U.S. utility companies in the design, construction, maintenance and operation of generating plant, transmission developments, costs of production and tariffs.

About three or four years later a senior engineer who had been one of the delegates described frequently going from one company to another who were in fact in competition.

He asked an American host why it was that they, the American companies, were able to be so free with their information knowing that the delegation was moving on to their competitors within hours.

The answer was that their technical development was so rapid that by the time a competitor had been able to verify the detailed information he might have obtained, and had been able to take advantage of it, the data would have become obsolete. This healthy attitude to freedom of information is badly needed in this country.

15. Nationalisation and centralised control

The Electricity Act 1947 brought fully centralised control of design, construction and operation for all UK generation, transmission and distribution plant and equipment. Due to the almost complete lack of new power station construction during the 1939-45 war the newly nationalised industry faced rapidly increasing electricity demand from both domestic and industrial consumers.

At first, in 1947, to speed manufacture and construction of new plant, turbo-alternator outputs were standardised by governmental order at 30MW and 60MW and so were their steam conditions (temperature and pressure).

This restriction was lifted in August 1950, enabling development of turbines of ever increasing individual output. New steam turbine outputs rose from 60 MW to 600MW by 1970 and later to 660MW.

In 1949 the first 60MW UK alternator with hydrogen cooling was commissioned at Littlebrook B power station. Better cooling had reduced the size of the set for a given output resulting in lower capital costs and easier transportation to site.

In 1956, at the Bold A power station, a prototype 30MW alternator using water cooling through the stator bars was the first in the world to do so. These and other technical developments were aimed at reduction of both capital and running costs. In each national electricity network there is a practical upper limit of generator unit size. For many years now the UK limit has been around 660MW. But larger networks such as in Germany and Russia are able to accept even larger units. In 1976 a 1,300MW single shaft turbo-alternator, the world's largest, was commissioned at the Biblis PWR nuclear power station of RWE Germany. The alternator was water cooled. In 1980 a 1,200MW single shaft turbo-alternator was commissioned at the 4,800 Kostroma (Russia) coal fired power station.

Meanwhile during the postwar period of system expansion the original 132kV transmission network required reinforcing at higher voltage levels. In July 1949 275 kV was adopted by the British Electricity Authority (forerunner of the CEGB) as the standard voltage for a new transmission network superimposed on the existing 132 kV grid and construction commenced shortly afterwards.

In 1965 the first 400kV line was inaugurated, running for 150 mies from Sundon, Bedfordshire to West Burton in the Midlands. The two new 275 kV and 400kV systems running in parallel with each other became known as the Supergrid. In northern Scotland the 275 kV and 132 kV networks act as the Supergrid. Again the whole object of their being is to reduce transmission losses and the capital costs of construction per MW. From the 1926 beginning of the national grid onward every effort was made to minimise visual impact on the environment, avoiding skyline intrusions wherever possible.

During the first 24 years of complete nationalisation the dominant engineer to emerge was Sir Stanley Brown. He became Chief Engineer (Construction) of the newly formed British Electricity Authority in 1949, later Chief Engineer. When the Central Electricity Generating Board formed in 1957 he became Chief Engineer and in 1965 Chairman. (This was an organisation twice the size of the next biggest producer in the world, the Tennessee Valley Authority.)

He immediately began a campaign to rush, in England and Wales, £100 million of new power station plant of ever increasing turbine size into commission. The first 300 MW sets were commissioned around this time on both sides of the Border (CEGB's West Thurrock and SSEB's Cockenzie). Fortyseven 500 MW units were ordered at a cost of £500 million (just over £20 per kilowatt). There were considerable teething troubles but Sir Stanley never faltered and went on to order 600 MW, later, 660 MW sets, with 1,000MW sets in prospect. Offered the Chairmanship of the Electricity Council in 1971 he chose to retire, aged 61.

In retirement he frequently wrote to the *Financial Times*. In 1977, lamenting once again the lack of political will which had prevented Britain's nuclear industry getting underway in 1970, he said

> "Make no mistake, the large scale development of nuclear power is both necessary and desirable. It is in fact inevitable unless either civilisation cracks or the world is prepared to carry on cooking over cow-dung fires and reading by candlelight. Nuclear power is ushering in a second Industrial Revolution and this country contracts out of it at its peril."

16. Nuclear power – its future as seen September 2005

Since the first commercial "magnox" nuclear power stations of the February 1955 White Paper "A programme for nuclear power" were commissioned in 1961, the Magnox and AGR nuclear fleets, together with the 1,100MW pressurised water reactor at Sizewell B have supplied 2,000 TWh of electricity to the UK grid. Today they are still safely generating electricity at the rate of over 80 TWh per annum, 23 per cent of total UK annual requirements of c. 350 TWh.

The last of the AGR stations was Torness, which achieved a world record for the longest continuous operational period by a nuclear reactor and turbine – around fifteen months.

The Sizewell "B" pressurised water reactor, was intended to be the first of a series. The Sizewell "B" Public Local Inquiry commenced its main hearing on 11 January 1983. The hearings were completed on 11 March 1985, the longest public inquiry ever held.

The station was not commissioned until 1995. The question arises as to who should bear the enormous cost of such public consultations. If as protracted as the Sizewell Inquiry, the engineering firms contracting to build the power station face heavy costs in maintaining reserves of technical staff, labour and materials to be ready to start construction if and when the Inquiry authorises construction.

It is clear that the public chiefly require assurance of the safe long term storage of all levels of radioactive nuclear waste arising from both "legacy" and "new build" power stations. Included in the same concerns must be radioactive arisings from medical and industrial applications of radioactive materials used for diagnostic and non-destructive testing methods throughout the country.

Revitalisation and dynamic reorganisation of national nuclear waste processing and storage facilities are unlikely to materialise as long as the government fails to enlist the support of their numbers of now ageing MPs still nostalgically reminiscing about their good old days as student campaigners for nuclear disarmament and their refusal to differentiate between atomic bombs and civilian nuclear power stations.

According to A. Rahman, (Ref 12) "The French nuclear industry is very active and contributes significantly to the French national economy. It receives full support from the French government and it meets its obligations fully by producing energy for national requirements. As France has no natural energy resources of any significance, it is viewed in France that maintenance of its nuclear power capability at a substantial level is vital. (As noted above French nuclear capacity in MW exceeds the entire present GB annual maximum MW demand.)

The French public is also quite sympathetic to the nuclear option. In order to maintain and sustain public support, France has undertaken a very substantive programme of R & D to resolve outstanding issues important to the nuclear industry. The lead given by the French government by issuing the Law No. 91-1381 is an indication of its farsightedness."

17. Privatisation in 1990 of the UK electricity supply industry

The Conservative government justifications for the 1990 privatisation are tabulated below:

The UK Electricity System

Prior to 1990	After 1990
Monopolistic	Competitive
Cost-plus tariffs	Downward pressure on prices
Engineering led	Market led
Centrally planned	Encourages diversity
Closed to new entrants	Open to new entrants

(*Electricity Association 1999*)

The main result was that both short and long term planning of new power station design and construction were to be left to market forces.

When the dust of this reorganisation had settled, putting it in military terms, the huge army of 150,000 people in the UK supply industry, with an annual productivity of about £70,000 per head, had lost both its General and its General Staff officers. Its Intelligence Corps – the CEGB Research Division – had also disappeared. Also, its assets had been sold off to private industry, including American, French and German companies. It now appeared to be a headless chicken, completely at the mercy of blind market forces.

By 2002/3, the total number of employees had fallen to 55,000 and productivity had doubled, to about £140,000 per head. The lights had still not gone out and nothing had changed – or had it?

What had changed was that in 1997 there had been a General Election and a radical change of government. In the same year, after the General Election, there had also been the UN Kyoto Climate Change Conference in which the new UK government had pledged itself to serious cuts in greenhouse gas emissions. (GHG)

Had the government set about implementing this reduction in GHG emissions evenhandedly among the factual generators of greenhouse gas emissions (including multi engined jet aircraft and rapidly increasing road transport) the subsequent impact on the landscape, especially the Scottish landscape, might have been greatly reduced.

But instead of walking to work at Westminster, or switching from 4 x 4 cars to minis, the government saw that the sitting duck, the headless chicken was at their mercy – the statistically transparent electricity supply industry, already showed a self started record of significant greenhouse gas reduction.

The idea of replacing or even increasing the non-GHG emitting nuclear generation fleet and simultaneously encouraging and supporting the re-organisation of the UK nuclear waste disposal organisation in harmony, as in France, never seems to have occurred. Yet the government were elected to run the country efficiently, not to bow to the perceived voting potential of emotional green pressure groups.

So GHG reduction by renewable energy was now to be by cheap(?) electricity generating windmills, thousands of them, and mostly in Scotland and Wales. To a government south of Watford it was a "done deal". But of course there was more to it than that. The UK national grid and its generators, which for fortytwo nationalised years had focussed on economy but also security of supply, without any competition, had been thrown to the market force wolves and non GHG emitting British Energy had nearly had to let the lights go out.

A growing electricity system subordinate entirely to market forces can not develop on the basis of short term "catch as catch can" investment. A secure source of long term investment is also essential. Market confidence depends on, et al, a government energy policy which can be seen to have been well thought out technically and once announced, seen to have been placed in competent and enduring hands.

18. Climate change problems

After the 1990 privatisation there followed eight years during which the industry was radically reorganised and sold to private companies, many of them of foreign nationality.

Then came a radical change of UK and government and the 1997 United Nations Kyoto Conference on Climate Change. in agreement with the internationally desired reduction of greenhouse gas emissions the new UK government launched a vigorous expansion of electricity production based on renewable energy and especially wind power, following existing Danish and German leads.

With forty years uneventful operational experience of large commercial nuclear power stations, over 20% of UK electricity continuously being supplied under base load conditions and free of greenhouse gas emissions, vigorous further development of nuclear power was seen by engineers as the logical and in the long term cheapest solution. By 1997 the jointly owned National Grid /Electricité de France cross Channel 2,000MW interconnector had been importing French electricity at nearly 100 per cent load factor for four years. Because France has few natural fuel resources of any significance (Ref:12) 75 per cent of French electricity is nuclear generated and greenhouse gas free.

Instead of instituting, as the French had done, an R &D programme to update and reinforce nuclear waste disposal in support of nuclear power expansion, it repeatedly over many years declared the "nuclear option" still open but did nothing to maintain it despite obtaining a second term in office. Instead under the UK Renewable Energy Programmes of 2000 and 2003 a huge programme of renewable energy, based mainly on wind power, was put in place.

19. Wind power and the pattern of UK electricity demand

Throughout the 1987 Edition "Chronology of the UK Electricity Industry" (Ref: 1) every event historically relevant to its development for around 100 years, amounting to some 4,500 items, has been indexed.

Only nineteen, less than half of one per cent, are under the heading "Wind Generators" and these installations include those in Denmark, Germany, Sweden, UK and USA. Some were as large as we see today. In 1941 a 1,250 kW Putnam wind turbine ran on public electricity supply in USA until 1945.

Until 1997 climate change and greenhouse gas emissions were not regarded by engineers as an issue. Wind generators were set up from time to time experimentally. The CEGB installed a 200kW wind turbine at their test station at Carmarthen Bay, upgraded it later to 300kW and planned a MW sized machine for Richborough power station if a suitable design had been available. Sweden installed a 3 MW machine in Gotland at about that time but neither appear to have been taken forward.

At that time the UK electricity grid was powered by fully controllable prime movers – steam turbines, hydro-electric and a dozen or so gas turbine stations from 1940 onward. All could be run up to synchronism and connected or disconnected to or from the national grid in a fully planned manner at will. Intermittent, uncontrollable wind turbines would not have been welcomed, especially as they were not seen to compete economically with existing conventional plant. The present programme is being heavily subsidised as part of the considerable price being currently paid for non-green house gas emitting generation.

Public electricity supply in the UK from the national grid has always allowed domestic, industrial or other commercial consumers to switch on and off at will, 24 hours a day, 365 days a year. The resultant aggregate national demand has long displayed consistent and familiar patterns identifiable by day, by season or by important public events. National grid control rooms have decades of experience in anticipating the forthcoming load for every hour of every day. The slightest imbalance of supply with demand is corrected by plant on standby or "balancing" duty. Fine tuning by ultra responsive pumped storage turbines is one technique.

The range of variations in demand, daily, weekly, seasonally and annually, is demonstrated by the following recently published graphs as follows:

Here the vertical axis is (System) Demand MW and the horizontal axis half hourly for 24 hours. There are four typical daily seasonal curves.

Figure 1: GB Summer and Winter Daily Demand Profiles in 2004/05

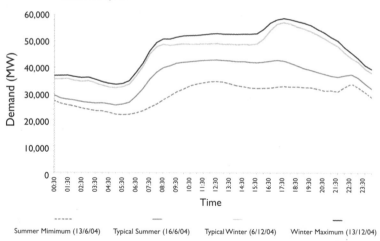

Reading from the lowest curve – "Summer Minimum (Sunday 13/6/ 04)'" from left to right, demand sinks slowly from midnight until at about 0600 hrs it has fallen to the annual minimum "Base Load" level. It then climbs slowly until plateauing at about 1230 hrs. Then follows another slow decline until, with a "blip" at 2230 hrs. midnight is again reached.

Figure 2: Weekly Maximum and Minimum Demands in 2004
(National Grid 2005 GB Seven Year Statement)

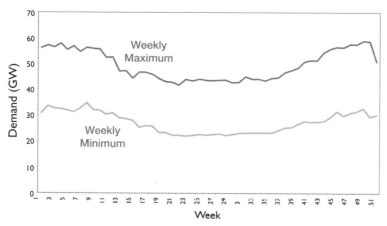

The next curve above (Wednesday 16/6/04), being for a working day, is more vigorous, plateauing at 0930 hrs and starting the evening decline at 1700 hrs. The upmost curve is the day of Winter Maximum (Monday 13/12/04) plateauing sharply at 0830 hrs, starting to peak at 1530 hrs, peaking at 1730 hrs and then declining fairly steeply away until midnight. That 1730 hrs was the GB annual peak 2004. To meet it required the Megawatt power equivalent of one hundred 600 MW turbines running at full load. In order to follow the subsequent evening decline in demand load 20,000 MW had to be shed fully controllably in six hours – an average of 3,333 MW per hour.

Figure 2 shows week by week over the year maximum and minimum MW demand curves. Figure 3 shows duration of load at various levels throughout the year. The right hand "tail" of the upper ALDC curve defines the MW height of the base load area and agrees with the annual minimum load MW shown in Figures 1 and 2.

Returning to our Figure 1 discussion of the Annual Winter Peak, the 60,000MW of steam gas and hydro turbines among which the annual peak demand is shared are connected directly to the

Figure 3: Annual Load Duration Curve for 2004
(National Grid 2005 GB Seven Year Statement)

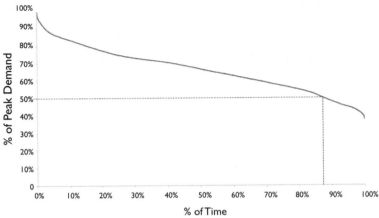

400kV/275 kV SuperGrid (275kV/132kV in Scotland) and directly brought on line and controlled by GB System Operator via a system of firm bids the previous day from generating companies plus a service from one or two dedicated power stations on "fine balancing" duty.

Wind turbines are not connected to the Supergrid but into the 33kV and lower voltage distribution networks as "Embedded Generation". Their output is not "seen" by the grid control except as part of a national or regional electricity increase or decrease in demand which must immediately be 'balanced" to prevent a rise or fall of system frequency from the standard 50 cycles per second.

Just how much wind power can be installed on the national grid without risking destabilisation and blackouts is still open to question. A debate in the House of Lords (Ref 14) concluded that expert opinions agreed that up to 10 per cent of wind generated MWh could be accommodated, but that there is some lack of agreement about the range 10 to 20 per cent and above.

20. Tidal power

The pattern of demand for electricity coupled with the huge scale of the industry makes it essential that proposals for large scale adoption of each kind of natural energy resources be preceded by thorough research into how their natural variations can be accommodated within the grid system due to the patterns of consumer demand.

As explained in Ref 9 (27.3.1) tidal power is governed by sea level which varies approximately with a 12.4 hour period, the diurnal ebb and flow cycle, superimposed upon a longer sinusoid with a period of 353 hours, the springs-neap cycle. The largest tidal barrage in operation is the Rance estuary scheme in France. The tides follow a two week cycle throughout the year. The output is computer controlled and optimised to match the needs of the French grid. The nominal average output of this 240 MW project is between 50 and 65 MW and is thus not the maximum that could be obtained, but it contributes maximum savings to the grid. While La Rance electricity is the cheapest electricity on the French national grid Electricité de France say that it would be too expensive to build any further power stations.

Studies have shown that the method of operation that results in the lowest unit cost of energy is either simple ebb generation, or ebb generation with pumping at high tide. As the generation period is about an hour later each day the generation (and pumping if used) needs to be planned in advance to integrate with the demand and supply of the grid.

21. Storage of electricity

The key to successful integration of natural energy sources with a rhythm incompatible with the patterns of consumer demand is of course storage of electricity. The only established large scale method at present is that of pumping water uphill. But this is only a specialised form of hydro-electric engineering, which tends to be very capital cost intensive. To visit the four pumped storage schemes in the UK viz. Dinorwig and Ffestiniog in North Wales and Cruachan and Foyers in the Scottish Highlands is to be impressed by their visual size.

But these four schemes total 2,788 MW – only 4.7 per cent of the GB 2004 annual maximum demand and, in a good year, yield for peak lopping duty about 2,800 GWh of hydro generation, less than one per cent of GB MWh total annual generation. To pump this water back uphill to the reservoirs requires expenditure of 970 GWh. Obviously any supplementary natural source of energy offering an annual increase of ten per cent would need the existing national pumped storage fleet to be multiplied by a factor of 5 in GWh terms.

22. Matching supply to demand (Ref: Section 18 above)

In section 18 above Figures 1 and 2 show, respectively, diurnal and annual (divided into week by week) consumer MW demand curves. The area lying vertically below each of these curves is the product of the MW average for each curve times its hours duration along the graph's horizontal axis viz 24 hours for Figure 1 and 8,760 hours for Figure 2, i.e. each area represents the amount of electricity in MWh demanded by that curve.

The mixed generation fleet in the system must continuously match the variations in MW (and therefore in MWh) of the demand curve 24 hours per day. If the average rate of supply (MW) falls short of the average rate of demand (MW) in any given period, the central grid control room is presented with a fall in system frequency for which it must immediately compensate.

This it does by increasing total *generation* MW above the total *demanded* MW sufficiently to cause system frequency to rise above the statutory average of 50 cycles per second *long enough to restore that average frequency over the period.* In such a situation voltage can also be affected but each alternator on line will normally have automatic voltage regulation.

This frequency control can only be exercised by the grid control room having at its complete disposal one or more dedicated "balancing" stations whose output is both completely variable and sufficiently responsive. In order of characteristic speed of response

Figure 4: Load Duration Curve showing responsive plant requirement net of demand management and firm contracts 2004/05 (National Grid 2004 Seven Year Statement)

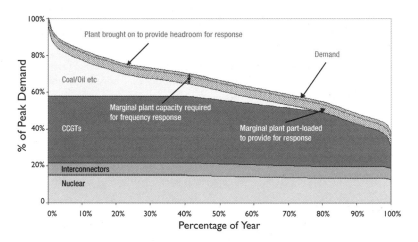

to load change we have hydro (pumped storage or natural flow), CCGT and coal fired stations. Two units of the Dinorwig pumped storage power station are customarily set aside for such duty.

It cannot be reiterated too often that the fundamental problem with large-scale introduction of wind energy, and other naturally based energy sources, is the incompatibility of their natural generation patterns with the daily, weekly and monthly patterns of domestic, industrial and commercial consumer demand.

Figure 3 (see also Section 19), the annual load duration curve (ALDC), shows the complete annual demand pattern by load duration and discloses the respective sizes of the base load (see right hand vertical axis) and load following components required to be met by the generation fleet.

Figure 4 shows how this is done by filling in the area below the ALDC with power stations grouped by fuel type in horizontal "layer cake" formation.

Acknowledgements

All illustrations were provided ex GB SYS 2005, on request to National Grid plc with permission to publish by Mr Duncan Rimmer, for whose prompt help I am most grateful.

I also wish to thank Scottish Hydro plc and Scottish and Southern Energy plc for permission to publish the graphs in Reference 9 below, including permission to annotate Fig 2.

I wish to thank Mr Ron Quartermaine, Convenor of the Professional Engineers Group, Mrs Helen Quartermaine for her kind hospitality, and PEG colleagues for helpful discussions.

Alan Shaw BSc CEng MIEE (retired 1981ex
National Nuclear Corporation Limited)
(29 September 2005)

References

1. "Electricity in the United Kingdom" (a chronology from the beginnings of the industry to 31 December 1985) : Electricity Council 4th Edition March 1987.

2. "The UK Electricity System" (an early description of the 1990 privatisation) : Electricity Association.

3. "Electricity Review 8" (Annually, Pub: May 2004 by Electrica Services Limited – earlier years by the since restructured Electricity Association)

4. National Grid Great Britain Seven Year Statement Copyright Information: (organisation since 1 April 2005 between NG and the two Scottish Transmission Companies).

5. National Grid GB Seven Year Statement 2005 http://www.national grid.com/uk/library/documents/sys05/default.asp

6. Public Inquiry: Proposed windfarm at Whinash, Cumbria: Precognition (18pps and Appendices) by Sir Donald J Miller FRSE.

7. "Energy systems and sustainability" Edited by Godfrey Boyle, Bob Everett and Janet Ramage (Oxford University Press/ Open University 2003).

8. "Renewable Energy" Edited by Godfrey Boyle (Oxford University Press/Open University 2004).

9. "Electrical Engineer's Reference Book" Edited by Professor M.A. Laughton and D.F. Warne: Newnes 2002.

10. Enterprise and Culture Committee: Inquiry into renewable energy: Submission by Alan Shaw 10 February 2004 http://www.scottish. parliament.uk/business/committees/enterprise/inquiries/rei/ec04-reis-sh awalan.htm

11. *Encyclopaedia Britannica*.

12. "Nuclear waste management in France" A.Rahman, Nuclear Department, HMS Sultan, Military Road, Hants, England. (This paper was first presented at an INSTN nuclear waste management seminar, France 18-22 June 2001)
13. "Digest of United Kingdom Energy Statistics 2004" ("DUKES") DTI.
14. House of Lords Science and Technology Committee "Renewable Energy: Practicalities" Volume I Report (pps 119-122).

APPENDIX 2

SUBMISSION TO THE ROYAL SOCIETY OF EDINBURGH BY
DEREK G BIRKETT

Investigation of Response Times for Standby Generation Plant

Summary

The introduction of intermittent sources of renewable energy, predominately that of wind resource, presents to the Grid Controller a challenge to accommodate fluctuations of output without compromising the integrity and stability of the National Electricity Grid System. The paper describes the circumstance of operation, the problems to be addressed and the need for a clear indication of intermittent capacity that can be accommodated.

Background

Government policy has introduced a system of subsidy to encourage the development of renewable forms of energy to meet obligations arising from the Kyoto protocol. A framework of challenging targets has been set that together with the terms of subsidy, effectively promotes a single source of renewable power for development, that of wind. There is optimism that wave energy will provide further resource in the future. Both these power sources are unlimited but by their nature intermittent and to a degree unpredictable.[1]

The most practical means to convert and transmit this resource is through the Electricity Grid System but this accommodation is subject to poorly understood technical constraints. The body of expertise in this area is surprisingly small.

The UK Electricity Grid System

Electrical power cannot readily be stored. The most effective means to date is by pumped storage, whereby water is pumped to a high head storage pond to be released when required. This conversion efficiency is around two thirds, has topographical restraints, storage limitations and high capital expenditure. Reliability and durability are prime considerations.

Grid operation has to finely balance the generated power with consumer demand. Any mismatch raises or lowers system frequency that by statute must be maintained between proscribed limits. The Grid Controller must continually instruct load changes to maintain balance, backed up by certain automatic and non-automatic features with varying degrees of response. Clearly this factor of response is of crucial significance. The consequence of serious imbalance is to reduce the performance of induction motors sustaining auxiliaries in power stations, thereby aggravating a deteriorating circumstance. (Appendix B). There are other forms of instability that can arise with the failure to maintain correct voltage profiles over the transmission system, leading to uncontrolled power flows and disconnection.

Much routine operation is uneventful but the incidence of fault, often prompted by adverse weather conditions, stretches the capabilities of the system together with its design and operational criteria. Statistical probability of failure, akin to roulette, has to be acknowledged. Understandably, the key ingredient of successful operation is predictability.[2]

Statistically the loss of supply to consumers from transmission related causes is extremely low but this disguises the severity of any failure with such a dynamic and inherently unstable system. The UK Grid system is much smaller and elongated than the interconnected system on the continent. This circumstance has considerable influence when comparisons are made with diversity and stability.

Wind Turbine Characteristics
The circumstance of intermittence raises a whole range of problems that are only ameliorated by reduced scale or aggravated expense. These are:

1. *Standby Power.* Sufficient standby generation must be available to replace or absorb power fluctuations from wind resource. This is above the requirement for coping with demand fluctuations and other generation plant loss. In effect, wind resource behaves as an extension of system demand with the important distinction that unlike demand, the direction of movement is largely unpredictable. German experience stipulates standby cover of 60% of wind capacity and this is on the large interconnected continental Grid System.[3a]

2. *Installed Capacity.* Wind resource cannot be factored into the requirement for installed generation capacity to meet maximum demands on the Grid System, either daily, seasonally or annually. Neither can it be relied upon for use as standby generation.

3. *Must Run.* In practical terms the output from wind resource must be accepted at all times. This is contrary to sound operational practice and creates the forced situation whereby the remaining generation portfolio must accommodate its vagaries. In the event of an island system being created under fault conditions, this characteristic presents an indeterminate delay towards achieving restoration. (There could be an automatic reclosure facility on wind turbines.)

4. *Load (or Capacity) Factor.* This is a variable figure and normally considered on an annual basis. Unpredictable variations are influenced by season, region, siting and whether onshore or offshore. Unlike continental practice, there appears to be an absence of high quality data in the UK with current wind output information.[4] Load factor is a critical yardstick of economic viability, frequently overstated by wind promoters. German experience indicates overall load factors of less than 20%.[3b] Given the preoccupation with targets, any shortfall of production implies a significant increase of capacity. In turn this would have implications for diversity calculations.

5. *Grid Codes*. There is the requirement for wind turbines, being all of international design, to be compatible for the UK Grid System. The problem of widespread tripping with induction machines, leading to Grid instability has been belatedly recognised in Germany but can be overcome with the expense of HVDC technology.[3c, 5]

6. *Volatility*. Continental experience has revealed considerable variations of output within short periods of time. Were these phenomena to coincide with other system fault conditions then grid stability would be placed at risk even with sufficient standby resource. The response time of this resource would be critical (Appendix C).

7. *Reliability*. Development of wind turbines has evolved since around 1990 and only recently have machine sizes been extrapolated to present dimensions. On the continent problems exist with blade and gearbox failure and the risk of type faults cannot be discounted. For reasons of dispersion, this item should not impact on Grid stability.[6]

8. *Governor Response*. All wind turbine installations to date do not have this facility, unlike every other significant generation source on the UK Grid System. Some development of this feature is under consideration.[7]

Transmission[8]

All wind farms above 20MW in capacity connected to the electricity grid require to be connected at a minimum voltage of 132kV to towers of lattice steel construction. With projected load factors in the region of 20-25% and Scottish targets aspiring to 40% of electricity being produced from renewable energy by 2020, some 7 to 9,000MW of capacity will require connection in Scotland alone. (To give some perspective, current Scottish maximum demand is around 6,000MW.) These numerous and dispersed sources not only need connection but also require the existing infrastructure to be significantly upgraded. The main interconnection between Scotland and England is already used to full capacity so that the implication of introducing additional must-run intermittent renewable capacity would be to quadruple the existing interconnection (Appendix A). The option of reducing conventional output to accommodate renewable production would be critically influenced by the rate of response this capacity was capable of, to avoid exceeding loading limits. In practice the interconnection could not be continuously fully loaded.

When potential for double circuit tripping is considered together with the level of projected intermittent renewable capacity to be installed, the future investment in transmission infrastructure can be seen to be of considerable scale. Such investment, above the future need for (subsidised?) standby plant provision to an already uneconomic resource requiring significant subsidy, some measure of the economic consequences arising from Government policy can be appreciated.

Operational Characteristics of the UK Grid with Wind Resource

1. *Governor Response*. A feature of all generation plant providing power into the National Grid is a limited, self correcting, automatic response to variations of system frequency. The absence of this feature from wind resource denies a proportionate correction to frequency deviation. At lower levels of system demand, in combination with inflexible base load nuclear generation, the must-run component of wind resource has a significant effect in denying this facility.

2. *Frequency Stability*. At low levels of system demand with limited governor response, in conditions of turbulence and a significant component of must-run wind capacity, serious problems of frequency control may be expected.

3. *Transmission Capacity*. The unpredictable variations of output associated with wind generation would be reflected with increased levels of transmission capacity to overcome problems of overload with line outages and fault conditions. This last circumstance would demand careful monitoring and

in situations where overload reductions were urgently required, the dominant presence of intermittent resource with its dispersed nature presents a problem of load reduction. Within the Scottish Highlands many applications for wind developments have already absorbed the full line capacity of existing transmission circuits.

4. *Line Losses.* The utilisation of full transmission capability and the considerable distances power will need to be transmitted from remote locations will result in significant power losses on the UK Grid System.

5. *HVDC Transmission.* This technology has a number of advantages to offset the problems arising from renewable development. Line losses are reduced, exposure to sympathetic tripping is avoided, and the environmental impact of overhead transmission is significantly less than for equivalent capacity with AC transmission. HVDC cable also offers an alternative routing strategy.

6. *Sympathetic Tripping.* A source of frequency instability that accompanies fault tripping of transmission circuits. Although being addressed within the Grid Codes, it has only become a problem by virtue of the increasing scale of development.

7. *Maintenance and Refurbishment.* The scale and dispersion of transmission infrastructure (as outlined in Appendix A) required to absorb the output of low load factor intermittent renewable resource, has to consider maintenance; another major consideration is refurbishment. Both these conditions introduce operational restrictions, with significant implications for costs and supply restraints.

Load Response of Conventional Standby Generation Plant

There are wide variations in the response times for different modes of generation and even within these modes. With thermal plant this extends to their condition as being hot, warm or cold but when fully established, ramping rates of 10MW per minute are common once the initial ten minute notice has been given but this notice can be reduced to five minutes. However bringing plant on from cold can take a full day to reach capacity output with variation to less than half this figure. When hot, a condition related to two shifting, these periods may be halved. An intermediate condition known as warm, can last for around two days with characteristics closer to the hot condition. These restraints, up to synchronising, are boiler related in order to raise steam but once the steam turbine is rotating, the constraint is to contain differential expansion within the turbine. Any departure from full load operation, the cost penalty of part loading becomes progressively prohibitive. Operation at minimum load cannot usually drop below a quarter of full load capability.

Synchronisation to the Grid System is a key step and load dispatch, though usually reliable, is not always secure. In conditions of frequency volatility, synchronising delay is not uncommon. Nuclear generation, being base load, cannot be considered as standby plant but it is relevant to note the ramping rates for load changes are very gradual and often exceed a full day to reach their full capacity.

Gas Turbines and Combined Cycle Gas Turbines (CCGT) have a quick start up response but are mainly located in England. This fast response would be a major factor to overcome frequency volatility and encourage increased levels of wind capacity on the system but this confidence may well be misplaced. Such a circumstance would introduce volatile power exports across the Scotland-England interconnection.

Hydro-based plant is much more flexible, with full load availability within ten to fifteen minutes, regardless of standing time. With pumped storage plant, designed for quick response, less than five minutes can be achieved for full generation but pumping response is far slower. However caution is necessary. Storage capacities usually have less than 24 hours of generation capability and machine operation is processional in that it is impossible to pump and generate at the same time. Once synchronised, loading rates can be very rapid. The UK has only four pumped storage sites with the installed capacity of one site at Dinorwic exceeding the remainder.

Accommodation of Intermittent Renewable Generation

It should be clear from the text that the ability to absorb intermittent renewable energy becomes increasingly more hazardous with scale. To secure the integrity of the Grid network, there will be an inevitable severe escalation of cost that will not be borne by the developer of renewable resource.

It was in 1999 that in evidence to the House of Lords Select Committee, the National Grid Company stipulated three conditions that would trigger significant extra operational costs. These were:

a) When installed capacity becomes greater than 20% of peak demand.
b) When subject to potential instantaneous loss equivalent to greater than 2% of peak demand.
c) When subject to potential loss over one hour greater than 3% of peak demand.

The analysis in Appendix C indicates these criteria to have been exceeded by current and consented wind turbine capacity, if the second criteria encompassing system faults is accepted.

The question arising from such revelation is at what level does cost deter additional intermittent renewable capacity and who determines that cost. Present structures diffuse this responsibility and indeed provide an incentive for compliance. However the problem extends much deeper to embrace the proportion of capacity required accommodating such issues as variable load factors, diversity criteria, onshore and offshore balance, location and future investment in other intermittent technology.

The introduction of major wind farm projects as on Lewis raises many issues that have a serious economic, operational and environmental impact. Together with the proposed 400kV Beauly to Denny transmission line the issues raised are of profound consequence and demand full enquiry. Are institutional structures adequate to contain these varied disputes and do they fully comply with procedures? Does a system of incentive provide the best technical solutions in an industry heavily influenced by strategic considerations?

Strategic Considerations[9]

The current direction of development, in the absence of any coherent energy policy, is dangerously exposed to cost escalation, distorted investment decisions and reliance upon a single unproven energy resource. An overview is required of other economic impacts affecting tourism and relief to poor households with no effective institutional voice to protect their interests. When local councils are considering any planning applications, the absence of any policy guidance denies the opportunity for strategic issues to be questioned in the planning process. Indeed there are proposals in place to deny such consideration as a basis for objection, in order to accelerate the procedural process.

As with terrorism, the long-term nature of energy resource requires cross-party consensus.

Suggestion

Were the Lewis wind farm proposal to become accepted, the output to be directly injected into the National Grid at Merseyside through a HVDC underwater cable connection. The advantages with this proposal would be:

1. An opportunity for the present day scale of wind turbine development to be proven in hostile conditions and a location having the most favourable load factor. This development presents a considerable technical challenge, as is recognised with offshore wind resource and the consequence of failure needs to be addressed.

2. The avoidance of sympathetic tripping and power fluctuations on the Scottish mainland system, having in consideration the scale of this development with both size of wind turbine and siting concentration.

3. A reduction of transmission losses over such long distance.

4. A reduction with the intended interconnection capacity throughout the northern Grid System of the UK.

5. The proving of HVDC cable transmission over such a distance. A cable of similar length has been ordered to connect Norway to the Netherlands. Operating experience would be an essential precondition before any contemplation of tapping the considerable renewable resource from Iceland and that before other European nations became interested with this resource. Having the cable in place provides a powerful option to obtain this resource that would be non-intermittent in character.

6. The undeveloped hydro potential of the North Western Highlands could complement the cable capacity of the Lewis development and give a more consistent output. It would also provide some assurance were the Lewis development not to succeed. (Current proposals require an HVDC connection, with its associated converter equipment, across the Minch.)

7. The HVDC link would avoid the need for the proposed 400kV transmission connection to Beauly from the Minch and re-evaluate the case for the Beauly-Denny 400kV connection, if only by delay. The consequence of future technical reappraisal to limit onshore wind resource could avoid the footprint of unwanted transmission construction in the Highlands.

To summarise, the suggestion would provide an insurance against any failure of the Lewis development and provide options for further reliable renewable resource to be developed.

DGB 22 August 2005

Addendum to Royal Society of Edinburgh Submission

Transmission p.2

On 22 July 2005 the Scottish Executive announced that the renewable energy targets of 40% by 2020 were in future to be expressed in terms of installed capacity and related to Scottish Electricity demand rather than generation.

A recommended assessment of 3.4GW of additional renewable power projects beyond those already built and consented would be required to meet that target, now expressed as a total of 6GW.

This reassessment is an inevitable consequence of the unsustainable criteria chosen with the original definition as outlined in Appendix A. While appearing to maintain the 40% target, in reality it represents an energy reduction to 60% of the original target. Installed capacity (GW) is an expression of capability only. The period of time that capability is exercised, otherwise known as production (TWh), is the only credible basis that can be employed if conversion to tonnes of CO_2 equivalent is to be calculated.

Definition

A generator of 1kW installed capacity if run for one hour would produce 1kWh of energy (a unit).

A generator of 1kW run for a year continuously would produce 8760kWh (units) or 8.76MWh.

A generator of 1MW run for a year continuously would produce 8.76GWh or 8.76 million units.

One thousand generators of 1MW (or 1GW) run for a year produce 8.76TWh.

Conditions

Scotland has an installed generating capacity of approximately 10GW producing 49TWh of electricity each year. A substantial export of power to England across a 2GW interconnection is additional to the Scottish annual demand of 34TWh.

Long term average of hydroelectric production each year is 4.5TWh from an installed capacity of 1.3GW.

Remaining renewable power assumed to be intermittent, must run capacity. (ie wind)

Calculation

Original Definition	40% of Scottish annual generation of 49TWh is 19.6TWh. Less 4.5Twh of hydro give a residual figure of 15.1TWh.
Revised Definition	40% of Scottish annual demand of 34TWh is 13.6TWh. Less 4.5Twh of hydro give a residual figure of 9.1TWh.

9.1TWH divided by 15.1TWh give a percentage of 60%.

6GW less 1.3GW of hydro suggests 4.7GW of intermittent renewable capacity.
9.1TWh is equivalent to an annual continuous generation of 1.039GW (ie 100% load factor)
4.7GW of intermittent renewable capacity would therefore require having a load factor of 22% to provide the revised target definition of 40% of Scottish demand.

A current estimate of Scottish wind capacity is 0.4GW that with a load factor of 22% would provide 0.77TWh per annum.

DGB 6 September 2005

Appendix 2a

Projected Interconnection Capacity Calculations with Assumptions

Current annual production of Electricity in Scotland is 49TWh. (This is in excess of annual demand as there is a substantial export to England through an interconnection of 2GW capacity.)

Long term average of hydroelectric generation is 4.5TWH per annum with a capacity of 1.3GW.

Estimate of current wind capacity is 0.4GW producing 0.88TWH per annum for an assumed load factor of 25%.

The Scottish Executive has an aspiration target of 40% of electricity production being derived from renewable power by 2020 that amounts to 19.6TWH. Subtracting hydro production gives 15.1TWh. This equates to continuous generation (100% load factor) of 1.73GW.

With an assumed load factor of 25% this suggests an installed renewable capacity of 6.92GW.

For an assumed load factor of 20% this capacity increases to 8.65GW. (Both these figures would include the current wind installation of 0.4GW.) An analysis of projected wind capacity in Scotland indicated a total of 14GW to be developed, consented and under consideration.[10]

Given the must-run nature of intermittent renewable generation, standby capacity at minimum load, minimum running of hydro and base load nuclear generation, the interconnection capacity required to export such power would need to be quadrupled.

This domination of a generation portfolio from intermittent sources, widely dispersed and subject to considerable delay were it needed to be disconnected, is a technical nonsense. It would imply significant fluctuations of export across the interconnection, wide variations of voltage levels and part of a general instability with frequency control. The cost implications would be severe, accompanied by a serious reduction with the integrity of the National Grid. Some amelioration of these difficulties would be achieved by a direct HVDC connection from a dedicated major wind farm facility to a major demand node in England, bypassing the interconnection.

APPENDIX 2B

The United Kingdom electricity grid system is independent of the far larger European continental system. However there is a 2000MW interconnection with France with virtually consistent import, but this is a DC connection that would only influence the frequency characteristics of the UK system by its provision of electrical power.

Supply and demand of power on the UK Electricity Grid has to be in balance. Any deviation results in an increase or decrease of system frequency that by statute must be maintained between certain limits. Grid practice is to operate within much tighter tolerances. There are various means by which correction can be given:

A. *Governor Response.* All conventional generating plant feeding the National Grid gives what is known as 'governor response', an automatic limited correction feature that reduces or increases power dependant upon the rate of change of this deviation.

B. *Load Dispatch.* The Grid Operator would instruct load changes to generation plant to correct imbalance. The degree of response varies with the generation source instructed and whether or not that source is connected to the system. Clearly some dispatch can be anticipated.

C. *Demand Dispatch.* Certain tariffs to industrial consumers enable disconnection to be instructed at varying degrees of notice.

D. *Automatic Dispatch.* When frequency deviation exceeds operating limits, certain rapid response generation (pumped storage) can automatically cut in.

E. *Voltage Reduction and Disconnection.* A further action that can be taken by the System Operator is to lower network voltages to consumers thereby reducing overall demand before a final option of disconnection.

F. *Low Frequency Relays.* Certain selected sections of the system can be automatically disconnected at pre selected values when the frequency falls, to reduce demand in stages.

A final involuntary consequence of frequency drop results in a reduction in performance of induction motors that sustains the auxiliaries of power stations, in turn reducing their output, so aggravating a deteriorating circumstance.

Imbalance of voltages across the system affect power transfers that in extreme cases can lead to voltage collapse and disconnection, so reactive control can be as significant as frequency control in maintaining grid stability. With such a dynamic and unforgiving system, once balance is lost, a very rapid fall into collapse can follow where time is of the essence and certain of the above corrections cannot be applied in sufficient time. Operator control is vital, in turn dependent upon communications to instruct corrective action and to receive information, essential to form judgements upon which decisions are based.

It is the huge inertia of the system that provides its resilience. An action taken in time avoids numerous consequential actions were the initial action not taken. Therein lies the problem of handling unpredictable power on any scale, especially in turbulent conditions. The assimilation of information has a time constraint that can effectively exclude all of the above Operator controls in certain situations.

The circumstances of major concern are generation loss without warning, tripping of transmission circuits and failure of communications. The effect of generation loss is enhanced at both periods of low system demand and daily peak demand. With low system demands the proportionate effect of generation loss is much greater and the nuclear base load component with its inflexibility far higher. At daily system peaks, available plant reserves are at their minimum. Transmission tripping can not only result in generation (and demand load) loss but prevent available generation from contributing towards restoration. The probability of such losses are considerably increased during periods of storm (and particularly blizzard) conditions. Nor should the effects of ongoing maintenance and refurbishment with transmission lines be overlooked.

Appendix 2c

Submission to the *IEE Review*

Stability Issues on the UK Electricity Grid

I would refer to the article 'Assimilating Wind' published in the *IEE Review* on January 2002 where the author suggests 8800MW of wind capacity could be installed before significant additional costs would be incurred on the UK Grid System (p12). His article makes reference to evidence submitted by the National Grid Company to the House of Lords Select Committee where three criteria would determine the threshold when intermittent renewables such as wind would be likely to trigger significant extra operational costs. The three criteria were:

a) When installed capacity becomes greater than 20% of peak demand.
b) When subject to potential instantaneous loss equivalent to greater than 2% of peak demand.
c) When subject to potential loss over one hour greater than 3% of peak demand.

Given his assumption of maximum demand being 50,000MW the first criteria suggests 10,000MW. The second criterion is discounted for reasons of dispersion and the third criterion suggests an excursion of 1500MW to be permissible. Drawing on the Danish experience over the first quarter of 2001 with 1860MW of wind capacity he then suggests 17% would be the maximum hourly power swing that translated to the UK would represent an installed capacity of 8,800MW.

What appears to have been overlooked is the potential for an instantaneous loss elsewhere on the grid system impinging with the third criterion. Extending the argument would reduce this installed capacity to 2,940MW.

There are three basic flaws with this reasoning. Firstly the article only makes reference to England & Wales whereas the Scottish grid system must be included (as it soon will be, under NGC control). For 2002 this system maximum demand is approximately 54,000MW. Secondly my understanding of the maximum designed permissible loss on the UK grid system for a single transmission fault is 1250MW and it may be slightly higher. It used to be 1000MW before privatisation. The third flaw is the reference to the Danish experience. On 29 October 2000 under storm conditions a wind output of 1715MW was reduced to 951MW over a one hour period. Taking the above installed capacity as 1860MW, this represents a swing of 41%.

Using the same reasoning as above but with the modified parameters the 8,800MW figure reduces to 3,950MW. If my proposition of the second criterion fault be accepted this reduces to 900MW. Currently the operating wind capacity is around 640MW with consent granted for over 2,000MW, half of which is offshore. What is significant is how susceptible these calculated figures become with variations of maximum system demand. With domestic electricity price increases of 30% being forecast, coupled to economic recession, a reduction in maximum demand cannot be ignored. For instance with a maximum demand of 50,000MW, the non predictable renewable capacity reduces to 3,660MW and 610MW where the second criteria is being imposed.

As a retired grid control engineer my instincts react against all thought of unpredictable renewable power on the scale proposed, sloshing around the system. Predictability is the key to secure grid operation. The Electricity Grid is a dynamic beast and unforgiving, it is inherently unstable. Wind resource does not provide any governor response to assist the automatic correction of system frequency deviations. Its exploitation on any scale would deter the introduction of new replacement capacity by soaking up available demand, the basis of payment within a market driven structure. At minimum levels of system demand with fixed base load operation of nuclear plant, in turbulent conditions, the control of system frequency would become a nightmare.

DGB 28 May 2004

References:

1.   Renewable Energy Practicalities: House of Lords, Science and Technology Committee. July 2004 (Report 1.11, 1.14 & 3.19)

2.   Power System Security: IEE *Power Engineering Journal*, October 2002, p241.

3.   Wind Report 2004: E.ON Netz GmbH. a) p3 &p9. b) p3 Table of Wind Power Statistics (Some allowance for incremental capacity introduced over the year is needed) c) p14.

4.   Workshop on Intermittency at Imperial College. Hugh Sharman, 15 July 2005, memo footnotes p2.

5.   HVDC Transmission for large offshore wind farms. IEE. *Power Engineering Journal*, June 2002 p135. Bringing Wind Power Ashore. IEE *Power Engineering*, Feb/March 2004 p33. Finding the Missing Link. IEE *Power Engineer*, Dec/Jan 2004/5 p28.

6.   A Storm Brewing. IEE *Power Engineer*, February 2003 p12.

7.   Control of DFIG Wind Turbines. IEE *Power Engineer*, February 2003 p28. Get ready to connect. IEE *Power Engineer*, Aug/Sept 2004 p30.

8.   Under Pressure. IEE *Power Engineer*, April/May 2005 p12.

9.   Costs of sustainable electricity generation. IEE *Power Engineering Journal*, April 2002 p68.

10. Gazetteer of wind power in Scotland. SWAP Report, January 2005.

APPENDIX 3A

COMMENT ON REPORT PRODUCED BY E-ON NETZ AT 14 NOVEMBER 2006

Investigation of events and failure of European Grid on 4 November 2006

Summary. At 2210 on 4 November 2006 interconnecting ties between the German E-On Netz control area and adjacent RWE Control area tripped, triggering a succession of further trips on overload resulting in three island systems being created across the European Grid. Automatic response and Operator intervention stabilised the island systems before reconnection 37 minutes later.

Prior to the tripping of the interconnection, a major interconnecting tie over the Ems river had been de-energised 32 minutes previously to allow the passage of a cruise ship on a pre-arranged outage. Previous studies had indicated an acceptable level of security would follow in the event of a double circuit fault being experienced.

Comment From the details of the report it is clear the system was being run to tight margins that would seem to be on a regular basis. Trading activity would contribute to this circumstance where the commercial imperative of avoiding constrained off penalties would deter a more cautious approach towards system security. Previous annual wind reports from E-On Netz have emphasised the transmission constraints within their jurisdiction and significantly, the extent of wind resource connection of 7GW having priority over more conventional generation. Such is the level of wind resource connected there are periods when wind output has to be constrained off. E-On Netz controls 40% of German wind capacity that represents half of European installation that in turn is 80% of the world's wind capacity of 41GW at the end of 2004. E-On Netz is therefore at the forefront of the problems facing grid operators to accommodate this intermittent resource.

Observation 1.(page 6) The outage of the Ems river circuit crossing for shipping would be an isolated event averaging three occasions every two years. The fact of only undertaking de-energisation would suggest a standing instruction to accept this condition rather than full permit issue. This is warranted given the system security limitations with such an outage and the need for prompt restoration. The notice given was more than adequate. In the event the outage was brought forward by three hours in conditions considered to be more favourable to the system. Full preliminary consultation had taken place between both grid controlling authorities.

Observation 2. (page 7) At the time of the outage within the E-On Netz control area, system demand was 13.7GW. Generation totalled 14.1GW of which wind comprised 3.2GW. Transit loads or traded electricity came to 7.3GW. Expectation of wind power feed in was on a rising trend to 4.5GW over 8 hours. There were single circuit outages on the system promoting grid reinforcement where simulation analysis had been undertaken. The situation was not unusual. These conditons suggest a significant transit load flow across their system.

Observation 3. (page 8) Immediately following the planned outage, alarms were received to indicate excessive flows on certain circuits. It is an indication of the tight operating circumstance that this condition was accepted. The internal procedures of E-On Netz permitted this condition, suggesting this had become a regular occurrence. Given the loading on the Landesbergen-Wehrendorf 380kVcircuit, it was surprising sanction was given to proceed with the ship transfer. Once this decision had been taken, the Operator became almost impotent as to future options in the event of changing load flows. In the light of subsequent events, the tripping of any interconnecting circuit would have prompted a critical situation, suggesting a flawed or inadequate simulation analysis had previously been undertaken.

Observation 4. *(page 9&15)* The conflicting overload limits between Landesbergen and Wehrendorf is inexusable and placed the Operator in an impossible situation. This is a clear failure of co-ordination between the office control authorities. Any operator would rightly assume his operating limit would extend through to an adjacent control zone. The fact of this anomoly existing and not being known about is an indication of the abnormal operating circumstance.

Observation 5. *(page 9)* A situation of alarm overload, potential hourly change of high trading flows and intermittency changes with high levels of wind resource, all combine to question the wisdom of allowing this ship transfer to proceed. The positive simulation exercise undertaken beforehand would have given a false confidence to the Operator, where the presumption of accuracy lay with the simulation. Whatever judgement or experience was held by the Operator, he had to accept the simulation result or be held accountable for trading losses.

Observation 6. *(page 9)* The load flow change following the hourly trading adjustment could easily have been initiated by wind intermittency and/or fluctuating system demand as could follow TV programme change. Reference to attachment 4 appears to indicate a rising wind output with one of the possible five wind plant feed in curves although this is uncertain and does not summate to the figure of 3.2GW. Analysis of attachment 5 & 7 indicate an increased demand of 5-600MW above forecast, not an excessive amount. The report is unclear as to how such change came about and reinforces the requirement to have controlled generation if system security is to be maintained with high levels of system utilisation.

Observation 7. (page 10) A heavily loaded system is prone to divergent voltage levels. The closure of a bus coupler at a major nodal point on their system could have had unforeseen effects in such a sensitive circumstance, especially if conditions were in a state of flux. The suspicion remains that any simulation exercise had not correctly monitored voltage levels. The possibility also exists of incomplete programming within the simulation facility.

Observation 8. (page 10) In the circumstance faced by the Operator, where time was at a premium, switching was the only available option. No analysis, transfer or load changing could have been undertaken.

Observation 9. (page 10) On such a heavily loaded system, once a major interconnector had tripped, it became inevitable that cascade tripping would result in island systems being created. The size of the *continental system* prevented much more serious frequency excursions and consequent grid collapse. It is a tribute to the operating skill of the various operators over the system that a unified grid system was achieved within such a short timescale.

Observation 10. (page 11) The shutdown of 2.6GW of wind resource on protection devices would have materially assisted the over frequency situation within the eastern sub grid. This was fortuitous. A similar level of collapse on the UK system would probably have led to system collapse. Annual E-On Netz wind reports have continually mentioned the problem of *sympathetic tripping* of wind turbines with system disturbances so such a scale of generation tripping cannot be seen as a planned effect, rather a consequence of over sensitive protection. This would account for such a high level of contingency generation (90% of installed wind capacity) having to be run by this utility.

Observation 11. (page 17) An important observation made in the report stated that 'there were no indications for any technical malfunctions of individual equipment or protective devices'. However care must be exercised in considering load levels at a precise value given the marginal changes as a proportion of the full circuit loading. A certain 'drift' can be experienced with measurement devices given their sensitivity.

Conclusions Given the profound consequences that follow from system breakdown, common prudence suggests it is unwise to operate grid systems at their designed limits. Not only was this being done, the evidence suggests this had been a regular occurrence by having standing instructions in place to accept circuit overload alarms.

Operator discretion was compromised by having a real time simulation facility that inevitably would overide judgement, particularly when the Operator could be held accountable for trading losses. An unenviable position.

Operating at the limits of the system only requires one maverick variable to bring disaster. This variable was the conflicting overload limit on the interconnecting 380kV circuit. The question remains with the situation that would have followed had a circuit tripped on fault prior to this interconnector. The eventual tipping circumstance could well have been a combination of increasing demand and (uncontrollable) rising wind output. Both these variables should have been anticipated. To say wind *intermittency* caused the shutdown would be misleading but nevertheless it introduces a variable that should have presented a far more rigorous approach towards contingency by reducing transfer or trading flows on their system.

The decision to blame the incident on 'human error' with the control room operator is perverse although inevitable in the circumstance. His position was untenable. The strategic overview must have been clear beforehand to allow the system to have been operated to such close limits. The probable outcome of the final inquiry will be to recommend additional transmission capacity, but this will still beg the question on how the grid system should be operated. What should be clear is the substantial additional cost to be borne by the transmission system in order to cope with the intermittency of wind resource.

DGB   1 December 2006

APPENDIX 3B

Observations with the National Grid Investigation into disconnection on 27 May 2008

Introduction. Government decision to target over 30GW of renewable wind capacity must have had confidence that the GB Grid system would be able to absorb this level of intermittent resource. The incident of 27 May, when an estimated 580,000 consumers were disconnected, raises questions whether this confidence can be justified. The need to establish the cause of this incident cannot be over emphasised and is an issue of major public concern with significant economic and political consequences.

Summary. This undated report is hobbled by addressing the concerns of BERR/Ofgem as distinct from a public need to address all issues relating to this incident. There is no indication that a final report will follow and significant uncertainty surrounds critical areas of information to explain the third loss of generation leading to consumer disconnection. No explanation is offered for the extraordinary series of generation losses and the obvious role of intermittent wind resource to influence this incident. Such is the emasculated role of National Grid, critical items of information have not been provided to enable a full analysis of events. So sensitive is the nature of this incident, no meaningful causes are explored or suggested. The recommendations made are limited to information supply from participants.

Generation
1. It is uncertain whether Generator A tripped or was shutdown with notification.

2. Was any preliminary warning given with risk of trip for Generator B?

3. No location or status of generation loss is provided, only capacity. This denies any analysis of trend, reliability or cause, however limited.

4. The role of fast acting response information with *pumped storage* is not acknowledged or detailed. This would normally provide an immediate corrective response with any large generation loss. There is an installed pumped storage capacity of 2.8GW on the GB system of which 700MW is located in Scotland.

5. The Scottish component of pumped storage would have been constrained by the border transmission limitation as described in 4.1.4 thereby denying any potential contribution towards frequency recovery.

Wind Resource

1. No reference is made in this report of *wind resource* becoming a defining factor for this event. The word 'wind' is not mentioned, only reference to distributed generation where absence of information from DNOs is acknowledged. (5.5.4). Paragraph 6.2.1 does state that this information is vital to explaining the full facts of the incident.

2. No meteorological conditions are given to suggest any variation of wind output or consumer demand.

3. There is no reference to 870MW of grid connected wind resource from Scotland being monitored by National Grid. (From the listed locations a figure 100MW less is suggested. Three attempts were made to establish if this monitoring was recorded.)

4. BWEA website indicates the GB Grid system has 2.3GW of connected capacity. The National Grid SYS for 2008-09 states 3.8GW although this is an anticipatory figure of which 1.6GW is Scottish grid connected capacity. England and Wales has no such Grid connection for wind resource where grid voltages are at a minimum 275kV.

5. A consideration affecting wind resource is the extent of *derogation* from recent Grid code modifications, given the scale of previously installed capacity.

Frequency Response (*fig 4*)

1. The third frequency drop from 49.14Hz as described in 2.2, 4.3.1 and 4.3.7 suggest a misleading drop of 250MW. However 5.2.2 indicates this as being tripped DNO embedded plant even though being two minutes after the second major *frequency excursion*. This third frequency drop suggests around 600MW of generation loss that has yet to be explained (5.5.4).

2. The operation of *low frequency relays* to give a consumer demand loss of 581MW as described in 4.4.3 and 5.3.2 is considered to be suspect. Has any corroboration of frequency conditions been sought from alternative locations? Even though governor reaction to a rise of frequency would depress total generation, instant demand loss of that scale would have expected a sharper correction (5.3.3).

3. With any severe jolt to the Grid system it is inevitable some tripping of generation plant will result, especially with non-synchronous items with low rating capacity. The difficulty of recording this effect on the scale required is logistically fraught, even though a requirement from DNOs (5.2.1). This circumstance provides a powerful argument against deploying *micro-generation* on any scale. Such tripping would be immediate in effect and not expected to influence the third depression with system frequency that comes two minutes later (4.3.7).

4. A component of pumped storage is normally kept in spinning mode (synchronised to the system) to automatically generate full load at 300MW with a drop in frequency below operational limits. Further pumped storage capacity called on manually could well have synchronising delayed by turbulent frequency conditions. This effect would also influence the automatic introduction of OCGT generation as described in 5.1.5.

5. Even though *consumer demand* for this period would be expected to be relatively static, the uncertain data provision as described in section 6 would deny any attempt at 'balancing' to establish an effect from a wind excursion. The recovery of frequency for the combined input of OCGT generation about 500MW (5.1.5) and the onset of demand control estimated at 1200MW (5.4.1) appears to be sluggish.

Single Event Loss

In outlining the framework of infeed loss risk at 3.1.3 the suggestion of normal loss at 1000MW is made with infrequent loss at 1320MW. This is misleading, as can be seen in Figure 9 where plant loss regularly exceeds 1000MW. A decade ago a loss of 2000MW was experienced with the loss of the French interconnection without breaching statutory conditions.

UCTE Recommendations

Following the Continental Grid incident of 4 November 2006, the technical authority *UCTE (Union for the co-ordination of the Transmission of Electricity)* in recommendation 5 of their final report required TSOs to have control over generation output with ability to start/stop units. For generation connected to DSOs, on line data of connection to be received by TSOs. The requirements for response of generation units with frequency and voltage variations, to be the same for both transmission and distribution connected generation, becoming retrospective.

In view of the absence of status from DSOs with distribution-connected generation for this incident and probable logistical difficulties with provision, the above recommendation should become a pertinent issue for future examination.

Analysis. The unexplained third drop in system frequency can be deduced from limited options. These are:

a) Consumer demand pick up (highly improbable with summer conditions)

b) Rogue loss of large-scale generation. In this event an omission to report a variation on this scale would be highly culpable and detectable.

c) Loss of small-scale generation. The consistent and even profile of descent after a settled period two minutes from disruption would not suggest this cause given the scale of loss.

d) Unusual variation of *interconnection* flows from adjacent systems. This option can be readily established from metered sources.

e) Recovery of *frequency (governor) response*. Expectation to recover in a shorter time scale from frequency stabilisation and prospect of being masked by auto start fast response generation (i.e. pumped storage).

f) *Wind excursion*. Given the weather conditions on the day (strong blustery winds) this presents by far the most likely explanation. The scale of uncontrolled wind capacity on the system (at least 2.3GW) to give a lull in magnitude as suggested would be entirely feasible, though random. Minor accumulations from some of the above sources could not be entirely discounted. Some indication of wind volatility could be realised with the monitoring of Scottish conditions (if recorded) by extrapolation.

Conclusion

The uncertainty with critical information surrounding the third drop in frequency prevents any definitive assessment with establishing the basic cause of consumer disconnection. Delayed and inadequate information from DNOs is not helped by a lack of rigour in not exploring the various options to account for this significant failure. Almost two months has elapsed since the incident with a report containing information that could be collected within days. The tone of the report is defensive, describes serious malfunctions of servicing utilities and whose recommendations are entirely focussed on information supply. This circumstance suggests an absence of authority with consequent inability to seek answers.

The knowledge of National Grid to investigate such incidents is unassailable. By a process of elimination it should have been possible to outline scenarios and suggest answers. This is not in the interest of any of the participants. As has been observed, nobody is in charge.

DGB   28 July 2008

Author's note

This comment was written as a response to the first report of the incident produced by National Grid. A second report was produced nine months after the incident with several detailed modifications. These observations were attached to the submission sent with Appendix 5D.

Beauly to Denny 400kV Transmission Line

SUMMARY PRECOGNITION BY DEREK G BIRKETT

Personal Statement

My residence in Perthshire has been for over twenty five years. I am a Chartered Electrical Engineer with a BSc engineering degree and a lifetime experience in the electrical supply industry.

Summary

The construction of this major transmission project creates an entirely new 400kV transmission line broadly along the route of the existing 132kV connection whose original purpose had been to connect the hydro resource of the Grampian region. Construction would also introduce significant extension of substation infrastructure at four additional sites above the destined locations. A fundamental rationale of the project is to exploit the renewable potential of the Scottish Highlands. Paramount among the exploitable renewable technologies available is wind resource, promoted by significant subsidy. This technology is intermittent and unpredictable having a perception of its absorption onto the UK Grid system as being almost without restraint. This is challenged, as is the need for significant extension northwards of the 400kv transmission network with alternative options becoming a more viable and prudent alternative.

Scottish Renewable Resource

A study commissioned by the Scottish Executive outlined the technologies available and assumptions with their exploitation. This study revealed some important issues that would affect any significant development.

Transmission. The study acknowledged the central role of transmission with any exploitation of renewable resource but considered the subject as too speculative and to be the subject for later study. What failed to be emphasised was the predominant influence of existing transmission to determine the location of wind farm sites. The most favourable locations with regard to load factor are essentially a secondary consideration. Given this context the suggestion of Local Authority resource allocation becomes flawed.

Load Factor. The study assumes a range of load factor for onshore wind around 35%. Extracted information taken from Ofgem returns over two recent years for Scottish operational wind farms reveal an average load factor of 30%. These same returns from the Renewable Obligation system of subsidy are the basis of a report used by the DTI to indicate regional load factors and are at variance with my calculated figures for the Scottish region. The detail of this circumstance has been presented in precognitions for the Griffin Forest and Lochelbank Public Inquiries. This DTI report reveals significant omission of data to determine national figures for historical load factors, only being rectified once Ofgem returns became available from 2002.

Predictable Renewable Resource. The only predictable renewable resource examined in this study was tidal flow being concentrated at the Pentland Firth and off Islay. Negligible amounts are indicated for large hydro and biomass, representing 3% of available resource. The estimate for large hydro is disputed.

Current Exploitation of UK Wind Resource

Recent figures taken from the BWEA website indicate an installed capacity of 1850MW to be operational, 710MW under construction and a further 3475MW of consented capacity due to become connected onto the UK grid system, giving a total of 6,035MW. The exploitation of a significant amount of onshore wind capacity was made available throughout southern Scotland by the sudden and accelerated approval by Ofgem of increased capacity for the Scotland to England high voltage grid interconnection. Active planning for further projects in Scotland total 2300MW (mainly over the Southern Uplands). This is under half of the projects in planning for Scotland and part of a 9,650MW total for the United Kingdom (excluding Northern Ireland).

These figures indicate a commitment for the UK Grid system to absorb 6,035MW of onshore and offshore wind resource with a further 9,650MW under consideration.

The significance of evidence indicating load factors to be less than forecast would have repercussions for future investment, particularly if changes were to be made to the terms of current subsidy. Recent reports from Spain, a major developer of wind resource, have announced reduced levels of subsidy.

The UK Electrical Grid System

Given that electricity production must always balance consumer demand it can be seen that the National Grid is inherently unstable and dynamic in character. It is important to recognise the limited size of the UK grid system when comparisons are made with continental conditions. Most renewable resource is intermittent by nature and unpredictable, none more so than wind resource. Each wind turbine is a potential source of instability that clearly must have some limit as to its absorption onto the National Grid. This limit has never been defined although some elasticity exists with increased investment with transmission and balancing generation infrastructure. Response times of conventional generation plant are a critical feature to cope with this instability.

Accommodation of Wind Resource

Political statements encourage the belief that unlimited amounts of renewable resource can be accepted by the UK National Grid system. Quite apart from issues of intermittence there are practical constraints circumscribed by the absorption of wind resource onto the Grid system at times of summer minimum demand. Energy cannot be 'spilled'. Levels of inflexible nuclear generation and supporting conventional balancing generation running at minimum loading need to be considered. There is the uncertainty of minimum demand, particularly with rising electricity tariffs, inevitable recession and more recently the encouragement of micro-generation. The consequence of significant scale with any micro-generation is that not only is consumer demand reduced, power can be back-fed into the distribution system thereby reducing system demand yet further. Even teleswitching of space heating load demand would not be available with summer temperatures. A technical complication arises with the failure to provide governor response, a first line reaction to changing system frequency. This facility is not provided from wind turbines, which are capable of wide fluctuations of power output over short periods.

The uncertainties with all these parameters are considerable. Nuclear closure dates may be extended, interconnecting ties for export with other systems may not be available and demand patterns could alter substantially. It is quite feasible for any wind resource in excess of 10GW to be faced with long periods of constrained off payments. When grid stability problems become an issue this figure becomes even less.

Intermittence Issues for the UK Electricity Grid

Operational practice demands contingency arrangements to be made available for remote possibilities. This circumstance is well illustrated by E-On Netz, the German utility, having the highest integration of wind resource in Europe where standing conventional spinning reserve was raised from 60% of installed wind capacity to 90% within a year. This was not entirely due to wind fluctuation but to the risk of sympathetic tripping from system faults. As a consequence, profiting from this experience, the UK has imposed stringent grid codes to mitigate this problem that developers have recently accepted, thereby being committed to considerable additional expense.

Evidence is accumulating from continental grid incidents where the intermittence of wind has complicated, if not influenced the causes of such disturbances. Denmark has curtailed future expansion and Ireland had imposed a moratorium with wind resource. Spain has reduced the level of subsidy. The recent European Grid blackout was initiated in the E-On Netz control area, Germany's largest provider of wind resource with a history of maverick load flows into adjacent control areas. A recent interim report issued by the European Transmission Authority has highlighted the lack of control with wind turbines, contributing to the deterioration of system conditions and delaying eventual restoration.

Evidence submitted by the National Grid Company to the House of Lords Select Committee in 1999 indicated the threshold of cost escalation to accommodate intermittence. This assessment is sensitive to variations of system peak demand. These conditions, as detailed in my main precognition, raise the question of coincident failure, especially during storm conditions when loss of large generating plant could coincide with loss of wind resource.

Uncertainties of Current Development

The example of grid code regulation illustrates an uncertain path when having to cope with significant levels of renewable resource where unprecedented technical issues arise for grid systems to manage. Other looming issues relate to governor response, ageing conventional generation plant, accommodation of low system demand and demand management control. These issues cannot be adequately addressed by advice from commercial interests that currently underpin the technical rationale of government decision.

The inadequacy and partial nature of technical advice lies behind Recommendations 4 & 5 in the Summary Report of June 2006 issued by the Royal Society of Edinburgh entitled *Inquiry into Energy Issues for Scotland*. Further uncertainty exists with Recommendation 20 to discontinue the system of Renewable Obligation Certificates supporting wind resource development and Recommendation 27 redefining the 2020 target for the proportion of electricity generated from renewable sources. A locational strategy and planning guidance is also suggested as with Recommendations

28 & 32. This Inquiry took evidence from almost a hundred expert witnesses with nearly two hundred written submissions.

Currently National Grid Transco indicates no foreseeable difficulty with accommodating intermittence. They assume an average UK load factor of 35% for all wind resource and have even suggested a 25GW level of installed wind capacity providing a capacity credit of 20%. This figure contrasts with German analysis by DENA and E-On Netz that indicates a corresponding figure, currently at 8% falling to 4% with planned expansion.

In their evidence to the House of Lords, the company stated two important caveats:

a) 'provided the necessary flexible generation and other balancing service providers remained available'. This condition being an area outside their responsibility.

b) 'the electricity market would need to incentivise the operation of a larger proportion of conventional generation with reduced load factors'. Another way of saying subsidy would be required.

The term 'capacity credit' can be misrepresented and can be seen in two entirely different ways. When viewed in energy terms (GWh) over an annual period, a figure can be arrived at, determined by its load factor. However in capacity terms (GW) with wind resource being unpredictable, a statistical approach towards availability would give a different result and if complete certainty were required, as would be experienced with extended periods of stable winter anticyclones, a case could be argued for a zero figure. Such calculations have an important bearing for plant investment when annual plant margins are evaluated for peak demands on the Grid system.

The continued exploitation of Highland renewable resource need not be compromised by transmission restrictions as fast moving developments with HVDC technology, present an option of transmitting power to load demand centres such as Merseyside or the Humber by undersea cable. Such an option would complement future exploitation of Icelandic predictable renewable resource. This technology yields a number of technical advantages that would limit cascade reinforcement throughout the northern part of the UK grid network and insulate the power source from frequency excursions and system disturbance.

A significant consideration among all these uncertainties would be the momentum of investment with both transmission and wind farm development, were a problem of system stability to arise. As in Ireland such a moratorium could be sudden and unexpected. Currently over 4.2GW of wind resource is either consented or under construction and with existing targets this figure can only increase. Any decision to approve a major transmission extension to the National Grid, as with the Beauly to Denny project, would have an extended gestation period to consider. The imposition of any moratorium or prohibition remains a distinct possibility, given the frequency of warning signals being experienced from utilities overseas where substantial levels of wind resource have been developed. This situation is compounded by the divergence of professional expertise with public concern for green related promotion.

Conclusion

Given such far reaching issues and uncertainties, the scale, cost and environmental footprint of the Beauly to Denny project represent an ill considered venture at this point in time. With reduced load factors for onshore wind, the scale of transmission losses and uneconomic connection, the justification for continued exploitation of Highland intermittent resource is prevented by grid limitations of system stability. This limitation must also consider the absorption of other developing renewable technologies of an intermittent nature.

DGB   8 Jan 2007.

Author's note

This precognition was produced for the Beauly/Denny Public Inquiry and was partly reproduced within the report of the Technical Assessor on page 72.

http://www.scotland.gov.uk/Resource/Doc/917/0088330.pdf

APPENDIX 4B

Beauly Denny Public Inquiry

CLOSING SUBMISSION BY DEREK G BIRKETT

1. Introduction

This submission covers technical information revealed during the Inquiry including the cross examination of five of the Applicant's witnesses. It should be read in conjunction with my precognition.

The timing of the release of documentation, its scale and the effort involved in accessing, analysing and absorbing information has been problematical for independent technical witnesses during this Inquiry. This has restricted my opportunity to cross-examine. It is unfortunate that previous material presented by me was disregarded on procedural grounds. Some of that material provided a necessary understanding of the technical issues. Throughout this submission I am conscious of the difficulty in presenting complex technical issues, capable of being understood by the lay reader.

I have attempted to ensure that none of the material contained in this document can be disallowed under the heading of new evidence.

The case for the Beauly/Denny line has not been substantiated. The proposal assumes that there will be no change to the energy mix for the generation of electricity or for the establishment of new generation in England closer to demand nodes. The proposal disregards the unpopularity of land based wind energy on the scale projected. The load (capacity) factors for wind resource have been exaggerated.

The Beauly/Denny project would exacerbate the problem of restricted transmission capacity at the Scotland/England border interconnection upon completion.

Proceeding with the Beauly/Denny line as a single solution when there are better options available is misguided. The alternatives to the Beauly/Denny line have not been fully explored. There will inevitably be changing economic, political and technical circumstances to affect generation and where it is to be located. The risk of this project becoming a stranded asset is high.

2. Limitations

2.1　　Scotland to England Transmission Interconnection

The realisation of additional interconnection capacity is not straightforward (APL 4/4 para 7.8.2). The justification for additional capacity above 3.2GW would involve a new tower line being built once the existing interconnection had been upgraded and reconductored from its present 2.2GW capacity (CD L16 pages 70/73). Such enhancement requires extensive works in northern England and constrained off payments would be high to justify new interconnection capacity.

The existing target of 6GW of renewable resource by 2020 based upon 40% of Scottish demand is highly susceptible to changes in demand and wind load factor as well as future direction of Government Policy. Recommendation 27 within the RSE Inquiry into Energy Issues (BDLG 10) indicated the target would be better defined as carbon emissions.

Any analysis of export capability when inflexible generation commitments are considered, indicates limited opportunity for wind resource expansion, particularly at times of summer minimum demand. Inflexible nuclear capacity of 2.4GW, contracted gas generation and balancing coal generation availability would need to be absorbed at a period when demand would be at 40% of peak, complicated by micro-generation having regulatory and subsidised support. (examination of Mr B　　). It is this circumstance with the limitation of interconnection capacity that prompted the re-definition by the Scottish Executive to consider demand as the basis of the 40% target rather than generation (addendum and sub appendix A within Appendix 6 of my precognition).

In cross-examining Mr P   the question was asked whether he recognised the border interconnection to be the major constraint in developing wind resource in Scotland. Twice I indicated the question had not been answered before moving on. It is essential that the Reporters determine whether or not the border interconnection is a major constraint in the development of further wind power resources in Scotland. I consider this is a major constraint.

2.2   Limitations within Scotland

The substation arrangements put in place by SPT at Denny would limit the 400kV component of the Beauly/Denny line to 1000MVA even though a circuit capability of 2810MVA was available (APL 5/13 para 10/1&2 and APL 4/4 para 7.15.2, table 7-2 and fig 7-1). This limitation would indicate the need for the Beauly/ Denny line not to be a pressing issue before 2020. Subsequent accommodation to provide increased power transfer capability towards the border interconnection would require substantial transmission infrastructure to connect into the 400kV trunk system across the central belt.

3. Quality and Security of Supply

3.1   Intermittence

One major component of system management relates to frequency control of the GB grid system. Due to wind energy being unpredictable, it represents a destabilising influence requiring responsive generation plant that is not the responsibility of the transmission provider (precognition appendix 9). There is an important distinction between generation response arising from demand variation and for wind intermittence. (The details of this circumstance were presented within my rebuttal paper).

3.2   System Stability

The extent of wind resource that the GB grid system could absorb is undefined and uncertain. Guidelines indicate the stage at which costs become substantial (sub appendix c within Appendix 6 of precognition). Mitigation measures do not remove instability; they only dampen their effects. Even this benchmark is open to contention with the prospect of co-incident failure, i.e. the prospect of a major generating set being lost in addition to a wind excursion. *My judgement, based upon practical experience over twenty years, is that the level where significant problems with instability can occur on the GB grid system has already been reached with the existing installed and consented capacity. This is in the region of 6GW of wind resource (appendix 3 of precognition). These issues can only be properly understood by a restricted category of experienced power engineers.*

Questioning of Mr P   established the use of intertripping with Peterhead and Longannet power stations that could have an economic consideration in addition to its security role. In examination of Mr B   his reference to reconductoring of the East coast interconnector providing improved stability, indicated the existence of a stability problem, supported by 300MW of increased capacity becoming available with the introduction of SVC equipment (CD L16 page 71). Mr L   gave assurance no such problem would affect the Beauly/Denny line. I believe the implications that arise from this stability problem need to be more fully addressed.

3.3   Intertripping and Boundary Conditions

An intertrip facility enables selective automatic control to be exercised where constraints under fault conditions could lead to circuit overload and disconnection. Detailed questioning of Mr P established two intertripping schemes affecting the SHETL system at Foyers and at Peterhead. Historically a scheme had been installed for the now defunct 250MW PFR plant at Dounreay where with only a single 275kV circuit, an intertrip to Beauly substation was needed.

Selective use of an intertrip facility would enable boundary security standards to be increased for N-1 and N-D conditions. The use of intertripping could be extended to avoid excessive constrained off payments for wind resource given the uncertain length of notice required to disable wind turbines, estimated at 45 minutes by Mr B   . Cross-examination of Mr L   indicated the effects of higher conductor temperatures enhancing circuit ratings would be limited to sag considerations and electric field tolerances (APL 4/4 table 7-2). Investigations to increase the north western boundary condition could exploit this relaxation as could reconductoring the redundant 132kV tower line between Boat of Garten and Tarland.

3.4 System Management

The scale of projected wind resource development north of Beauly is outlined in APL 4/2 and APL 4/5 in tables 3.9 and 3.10 indicating 3.2GW and 5.4GW. Evidence of a further 4.4GW is revealed for the SPT area in BDLG 18 at 2.4.5. The 3.2GW and 4.4GW figures are supported by evidence from the BWEA (appendix 3 of my precognition). This focussed scale of wind resource development introduces serious and unmanageable problems for system management with no indication of how such a scale of wind resource is to be managed (elaboration of these issues was contained within my rebuttal paper that was not accepted).

4. Alternative Schemes

References to HVDC subsea cable alternatives in the SKM report and PB Power proposals (APL 5/15 and 5/18) explored a number of alternative destinations in both Scotland and England. This technology is favoured by distance and would bypass the constraints of the border interconnection and insulate wind resource from system disturbance and frequency excursion. Offsetting costs for additional trunk capacity from Denny to the point of destination in middle England, do not appear to have been included. Cross-examination of Mr B   revealed the basis of HVDC cost comparison in his precognition (section 10.5) to be inconsistent with the Applicant's proposal for the Beauly Denny transmission line where winter post fault continuous rating values were being compared to all-year-round capability. These issues are significant and would dilute the argument for the Beauly/Denny proposal.

The option of an undersea cable as an alternative to the Applicant's proposal for the Beauly/Denny line is raised in my precognition. Both projects represent an inflexible five-year commitment. A significant portion of my precognition outlined the uncertainties and cost escalation arising from future increasing scale with wind resource development. Questioning indicated the technical issues arising from Recommendation 5 of the European UCTE final report into the recent European Grid failure, the implications of which remain to be addressed for wind resource upon the GB Grid system. The East Coast proposal submitted by Sir   , differed significantly from the Applicant's East Coast alternative, presenting a staged development that avoided becoming hostage to changed circumstance, technical, economic and political. I have examined the boundary conditions in Sir   's proposal and am satisfied this proposal presents a viable option, having further studied the Applicant's supporting documentation.

The provision for harvesting along the length of the Beauly/Denny line represents a substantial cost component of the overall project. Questioning of Mr B   suggested significant cost savings could be made if a single grid voltage could be maintained along the route of the line at the four grid substations affected, thereby avoiding an investment of seven grid transformers.

5. Balancing Hydro and Pumped Storage

In cross-examination of Mr B   the suggestion was made that 250MW of Northern hydro was available for two-thirds of the year in conjunction with 300MW of pumped storage to manage intermittent wind resource and provide consistent output for specified periods, subject to dedicated purpose and appropriate financial inducement. This compared with the Applicant's estimate of 125MW for hydro and 100MW with pumped storage. By returning 27MW of reduced plant capacity at five locations, previously derated for commercial purposes, a significantly higher level of hydro flexibility can be achieved. A further 100MW of all year round hydro would become available once the scheme at Glen Doe is commissioned.

A similar suggestion put to Mr B   suggested 250MW of all year round hydro in the southern SHETL area could be combined with 400MW of pumped storage at Cruachan to provide consistent output with wind resource. A new substation at Inverarnan would facilitate this proposal (P   precog 8.5 and 8.7).

Such use of hydro resource would alleviate many problems associated with wind intermittence. Not only would these arrangements alleviate boundary conditions, it would provide much needed stability for the grid management of the transmission system, mitigating the instability that would arise with excessive power flows across the border interconnection (these issues had been developed further within my rebuttal paper).

6. Plant Margin Assessment

Evidence presented within my precognition and questioning of Mr B   revealed much lower load (capacity) factors for wind resource than previously assumed. Recent reports have confirmed these findings. This revelation has far-reaching consequences. Capacity credit is a probabilistic figure given as a percentage of installed wind capacity that can be considered as firm capacity for the purpose of plant scheduling. Its value is significantly affected by load factor. As a component of the overall plant mix it would have a disproportionate effect upon the traditional 20% value for the annual plant margin assessment for contingency reserve with significant implications for generation investment. This is bound to reflect in any economic assessment of wind resource (BDLG 25 Exec Summary items 20-28).

7. Conclusion

The proposal is based upon flawed assumptions relating to the ultimate capacity and performance of wind energy. The Beauly/Denny project would exacerbate rather than alleviate the problem of restricted capacity at the border interconnection upon completion. The case for this line has not been fully substantiated. The proposal assumes unlimited exploitation of renewable resource and fails to address the implications that arise from reduced load (capacity) factor for wind resource. The alternatives to the Beauly/Denny line have not been fully explored, the most significant of which is the east coast option. Quality and security of supply issues have not been fully addressed. Intermittency is a serious issue and while the dedicated use of hydro and pumped storage can assist, it cannot fully address the unmanageable effects of wind energy. To proceed with the Beauly/Denny project would aggravate the problem of restricted capacity at the Scotland/England border interconnection upon completion while for the duration becoming hostage to changing circumstance, technical, economic and political. The risk of a stranded asset must be high and unacceptable.

4 May 2007

Author's note

This closing submission brought together issues arising from questioning of the Applicant's witnesses during the the strategic session of the public inquiry. The names of individuals have been removed.

Appendix 4C

Assessment of the Grid Connection Options for the Scottish Islands

Introduction

In mid June 2007 a report by consultant TNEI was issued (date of publication 27 March) commissioned by Highlands and Islands Enterprise (HIE) in conjunction with the Scottish Executive and Island Councils. This 129-page document made recommendations for connecting renewable resource from the Western Isles, Orkney and Shetland to the mainland grid network. Reference was made to developments having a clear association with such connections. These included a projected HVDC link between Scotland and Norway, the proposed offshore Beatrice project and significantly an HVDC connection from Peterhead to Eastern England, thereby augmenting the HVAC border interconnections between Scotland and England.

This report was accepted by the Highland Council on 28 June and would arguably have had a significant effect if presented to the Strategic session of the Beauly/Denny Public Inquiry that ran from 6 February to 11 May. An important observation was the restriction to develop renewable resource in Scotland presented by existing cross-border interconnection capacity (pages 16-17).

This paper brings together evidence presented during the Inquiry and attempts to provide a strategic and operational perspective that would diminish the relevance and cost effectiveness of the proposed Beauly to Denny project.

Strategic Considerations

Structural. Historically the decision making process has been driven by artificial market signals with uncertainty in the absence of a long-term strategic perspective. The pivotal role of Ofgem as financial guardian, influenced by Government policy, has its assessment role effectively denied scrutiny by recent decisions of the Scottish Executive, relating to legal objection within the Beauly/Denny Public Inquiry. Further complication arises when investment decision becomes reliant upon 'constrained off' payment where operational assumptions assume a significant component of cost justification.

Renewable Resource. The Scottish Islands present the highest load factor of wind resource within the UK. Its exploitation is largely dependant upon HVDC connection where high capital cost of converter equipment influence the economic case for development. If combined with other renewable resource to improve the cable utilisation factor, the economic case becomes transformed. This could arise with other localised renewable resource (such as wave generation), a Scotland to Norway interconnection as already investigated (page 39) and even an Icelandic connection where considerable hydro and geothermal potential is available.

Intermittency. A problem that arises with exploitation of renewable resources is the unpredictable nature of production. This condition imposes constraints upon the Electricity Grid, having an economic dimension with the level of intermittent capacity capable of being absorbed to avoid the onset of instability. Power supplied through an HVDC connection is insulated from system instability, enabling additional renewable resource of an intermittent nature to be fed onto the GB Grid system.

The level of intermittent renewable capacity that can be safely managed upon the GB Grid system is currently undefined. This consideration must have in mind the existing and consented resource for connection, the balance of various intermittent technologies, load factor, diversity, and cost. Current direction of policy assumes an almost limitless exploitation.

Alternative Interconnection. The report suggests an alternative means of exporting Scottish generation South to England by a connection between Peterhead and Hawthorn Pit (Hartlepool) or Walpole (Wisbech) (p53 to 57). This proposal bypasses the existing cross-border interconnection, avoids the pipeline concentration at St Fergus and would limit the extensive transmission reinforcement required throughout Northern England and Central Scotland, were it found necessary to provide a third cross-border HVAC interconnection. The need for the projected Beauly/Denny 'upgrade' is avoided, as a strong connecting link already exists along the Grampian East Coast, capable of being upgraded to 400kV operation. However substantial reinforcement between Beauly and Peterhead would be required that is envisaged under future NGT SYS proposals.

By suitable modification of the proposal submitted by Sir   during the Beauly/Denny Public Inquiry, it would be feasible to provide a strengthened connection between the central belt and Beauly without the five-year commitment of the Beauly/Denny 'upgrade'. This enables programmed flexibility for the installation of an HVDC connection to England. Other possible generation projects require consideration with carbon sequestration at Peterhead, offshore wind development and provision of nuclear capacity at Stakeness. The suggested 400kV double circuit line between Beauly and Keith would require a further 400 kV upgrade from Keith to Kintore. It may even be appropriate for Kintore to be the source location for the HVDC interconnection instead of Peterhead thereby avoiding the pipeline complex at Cruden Bay.

Operational Considerations. A major concern arising from continued renewable development in Scotland is overload of the Scotland/England interconnection, particularly with extensive uncontrolled generation connected to the Scottish system. This is not confined to thermal limitations but extends to known stability problems. Dedicated operation of hydro and pumped storage can alleviate this concern to an extent but an HVDC connection would allow a controlled flow facility, enabling a responsive means of avoiding overload on the HVAC border interconnection. Without such response lower export levels would be necessary and constrained off payments more prevalent. System operation has to consider fault and maintenance scenarios with their consequent constraints and additional flexibility from a controlled HVDC connection would provide substantial economic benefit.

Harvesting. A significant factor justifying the Beauly/Denny 'upgrade' is the potential for harvesting. Alternative means to access potential sites are available by adapting the 275kV Foyers spur and promoting the Inverarnan substation in Argyll with double stringing of the 132kV circuit connection between Errochty and Killin. Avoiding additional grid voltages at four substation locations along the length of the proposed line would enable significant cost savings to be made.

Conclusion

The TNEI Report presents a considered proposal to develop the renewable potential of the Scottish islands and outlines the many regulatory, environmental and commercial considerations that need examination in addition to the technical issues. Detailed scrutiny of HVDC alternatives identifies a proposal that in conjunction with an East Coast alternative presented at the Beauly/Denny Public Inquiry, accommodates requirements for renewable development in the Highlands and avoids the environmental degradation implicit with the proposed Beauly/Denny 'upgrade'. The impact of this study, had it been presented at the strategic session of the public inquiry, would have been considerable and questions need to be asked as to why this evidence did not become available.

Derek G Birkett
3 August 2007

Author's note

This response was sent to the Energy Minister of the Scottish Government after the close of the strategic session of the public inquiry, based upon a delayed report by TNEI consultants.

Appendix 5A

Submission to the House of Lords Select Committee on Economic Affairs

The Economics of Renewable Energy

Introduction

1. My name is Derek George Birkett. I am a graduate and chartered electrical engineer having a lifetime of experience within the electrical supply industry and resident in the Scottish Highlands for thirty-eight years. My initial training and employment with the CEGB in Yorkshire was with coal based generation, progressing onto project installation and commissioning at five power station locations, three of which were nuclear. In the mid seventies I moved into hydro generation then Grid system operation with the North of Scotland Hydro Electric Board before retiring in 1999 as shift System Control Engineer. All my employment has been in the nature of direct practical application.

2. Over the last two years I have actively opposed renewable development at three Public Inquiries. The first two with wind farm applications at Griffin and Lochelbank in Perthshire and the last as one of two independent witnesses for the strategic session of the Beauly-Denny Public Inquiry into a 400kV transmission line application.

3. The evidence I wish to present is submitted on an individual basis. There is a substantial annexe component included with material taken from the above public inquiries. This is preceded by a submission made to the Royal Society of Edinburgh for their Inquiry into Energy Issues for Scotland. The scope and complexity of technical issues make it difficult to offer statements without verification but to limit my

submission to a manageable length, many appendixes have not been included.

4. In opposition to these developments, my motivation has been the impact on the local environment and knowledge of the destabilising effect that projected wind resource would have on the GB Grid system. This has been reinforced by the perceived excessive overall cost and unease with the political justification for renewable policy.

Evidence for Interconnection

5. Throughout the evidence contained in the Annexes it has been assumed that the basic integrity of the GB Grid system would be maintained as a self-contained entity. This assumption can no longer be maintained in the light of recent developments. The means of fully coping with intermittence show no indication of being reinforced except by increased interconnection with the continental grid. This may well be a commercial solution in that an alternative use for trading exists but in so doing a one-way dependency on the continental grid is created. This may well be unacceptable for political, strategic and security considerations.

6. With increasing intermittent renewable generation capacity, primarily wind resource, being introduced onto the GB Grid system, the expected means to accommodate this additional intermittence would be shared by a larger proportion of spinning reserve, supported by generation plant with fast reacting response, such as Open Circuit Gas Turbines (OCGT) or hydro-electric pumped storage schemes. A recent Ofgem/Berr report (reference 1) suggests no increased capacity for this category of generation while indicating a significant increase of interconnection capacity around 2010 (figure 1).

7. Current HVDC interconnection capacity with the GB Grid system has a 2GW connection from France and a 450MW connection between Northern Ireland and Scotland. A

projected 1300MW interconnection with the Netherlands is indicated within the National Grid SYS statement.

8. There has been a recent announcement by National Grid and Elia (Belgium transmission system operator) to study the potential for a 700-1300MW interconnection (reference 2).

9. An all-Ireland study into investment for renewable development would double the existing 450MW interconnection from Scotland to 1GW, with fast acting generating plant also contemplated. Part of their problem with intermittence would then be passed onto the GB Grid system (reference 3).

10. An assessment of Grid connection options for the Scottish Islands proposed a Norwegian interconnection that could tap the high load factor wind resource potential of Shetland (reference 4). (This report provides detailed options for subsea cable connection to England.)

11. The recent government decision to promote a UK nuclear programme from continental suppliers would suggest reactor sizes to be in excess of existing construction. This would expect to increase the requirement for fast response plant. The questionable option of promoting interconnection as a substitute solution remains.

Hydro Electric Development

12. From a technical standpoint hydroelectric generation with storage has the most attractive features of any energy resource and its limited exploitation arises from the significant capital outlay required that is essentially a long-term investment. The scale of potential resource within the Scottish Highlands reflects existing development and its exploitation would provide an ideal operational complement with any intermittent resource (reference 5).

Perspective of Approach

13. System operation demands a predictable framework for efficient operation. There should be a presumption against the introduction of uncontrollable generation onto the GB Grid system. The situation that currently exists imposes on the Grid authority technical adaptation leading to inefficient operation, complexity and cost. Although accommodation can be made, no single body is responsible to make overall technical and cost judgements to prevent excessive and distorted decisions from being implemented.

14. All these technical measures are essentially a response to overcome potential instability that must question just how essential is this policy justification. Grid integrity is being sacrificed to accommodate unpredictable and uneconomic generation whose capacity must be almost replicated with alternative firm generation. Any scale of renewable development undermines the economic basis of such standby capacity. A structural impediment is being introduced to what purpose and advantage?

Evidence within Annexes

15. Annexe 1 presented as evidence to the Royal Society of Edinburgh, investigates the response times of standby generation plant and describes the circumstance of Grid operation. Appendix A reveals the unsustainable targets promoted by the Scottish Executive while Appendix C was a published letter in response to a prominent article in the technical press advocating wind development (reference 6).

16. Annexe 2 examines the issue of wind resource load factor as presented in a precognition for the Lochelbank Public Inquiry. It updates similar evidence as given to the Griffin Public Inquiry in July 2006. The evidence reveals excessive estimates for carbon saving and provides actual energy production details from all Scotland wind projects. Only appendixes 5 and 11 have been included.

17. Annexe 3 is a precognition for the Beauly to Denny Public Inquiry questioning the scale of intermittent wind resource capable of being absorbed onto the GB Grid system. This issue would impact on the assumptions made to justify not only the Beauly to Denny transmission line but with supporting substation infrastructure along its route. Intermittence issues are explored, as are future uncertainties. Appendix 7 and 12 are included. Appendix 6 is identified as Annexe 1 above. The closing submission is also presented.

18. Annexe 4 is in two parts. A Summary paper was judged necessary for clarity when presenting this Rebuttal paper in the course of the Beauly/Denny Public Inquiry. These documents were submitted but not accepted by the Reporters.

List of References

1. Transmission Access Review – Interim Report. 76 pages. Ofgem (08/08) BERR(URN 08/609). 31 January 2008.
2. *Engineering & Technology*. IET Journal Page 13. 23Feb-3Mar 2008.
3. An Island Grid Study. 16 pages. Irish Dept of Communications, Energy and Natural Resources. January 2008.
4. TNEI Report. Assessment of the Grid Connection Options for the Scottish Islands. 129 pages. Highlands and Islands Enterprise. 27 March 2007.
5. Review of potential hydroelectric development in the Scottish Highlands. *Electronics and Power*. Pages 339-346. (IEE journal). May 1979.
6. Feedback. *IEE Review*. Page4. July 2004. Response to article 'Assimilating Wind' by David Milborrow. *IEE Review*. Page 9-13. January 2002.

Derek G Birkett   20 May 2008

Author's note

Submision to the House of Lords Inquiry on the Economics of Renewable Energy presenting evidence of proposed interconnections to other grid systems (Evidence page 231). Since the Inquiry, approval has been given for a further Irish 500MW HVDC interconnection from Co Meath to Deeside.

APPENDIX 5B

Response to Renewable Energy Consultation

Introduction

The author has had a lifetime of experience as a chartered engineer in the electrical supply industry and on retirement held responsibility for the operational control of the Grid system in the North of Scotland. This direct experience, with expertise limited to only a few score individuals across the United Kingdom, is pivotal in establishing the practical case whether wind resource on the scale proposed can be technically sustainable on the GB Grid system. There are also other technical issues imperfectly understood and where resolution comes with increased cost, a factor often neglected with renewable development. The basic concern with energy is not so much its provision but its cost.

Information Background

The nature and complexity of electrical supply is such that direct control by any outside agency would become impossible without consent. With privatisation, shareholder interest became the defining consideration and information supply to outside agencies, including government, would always be tempered by this reality. Confidence to release information also has a part and past events define this level of cooperation. The introduction of significant subsidy distorts any sense of wider responsibility when shareholder interest is affected. The problem asserted lays not so much with the information given, more in what is withheld.

This background defines the quality of information used to establish Government Policy. Professional bodies are not immune to these pressures and increasingly recourse to public consultation is being taken. This taps the knowledge and experience of retired professionals who are no longer constrained by company coercion but nevertheless can have residual loyalties. International comparisons while providing useful avenues for technical study, need close examination to be relevant in a national context. A problem may arise with the lack of technical knowledge and experience within the civil service and parliamentary research staff to correctly interpret the complex technical information presented. This is turn could impact on the development of a sound Government energy policy.

Technical Issues affecting Grid system stability

Response Capability

Renewable energy by its nature is intermittent (except for large scale hydro) and provision for standby generation must be made. With wind becoming the prominent renewable resource, initial estimates had suggested up to 20% of installed capacity could be considered firm, based upon an average load factor of 35%. Calculations from Ofgem returns over a five-year period now indicate a value of load factor closer to 25-26%. This significant change has prompted an industry source to consider 8% as a more realistic figure as a firm supply contribution to meet winter peak demand. This has an influence with the proportion of installed wind capacity to be covered by standby generation that is in the order of 80% and above. The resource most suited for this application is flexible coal-fired generation, virtually all of which is currently in excess of thirty-five years of age, having been constructed for a design life of thirty years.

Since privatisation in 1990 the only significant capital investment decision for supply has been with gas turbine generation, highly susceptible to fuel supply costs in a volatile market, only recently exposed to global trading conditions from declining North Sea gas. With increasing regulation and intervention by the State, coupled to an imposed and changing subsidy (currently funded by 8% on consumer bills), this has created an uncertain investment climate, promoting short-term response for relatively low capital cost generation with brief construction timescales. A consideration with gas supply is that with any restriction, for obvious safety reasons, supplies to the domestic consumer must always have priority. Another concern relates to excessive load cycling arising from increasing intermittency on the Grid system with consequent increase in maintenance outages, reduced reliability and operating life.

Pumped storage has long been an effective and reliable tool for system balancing with immediate and significant response. However capital costs are high and conversion efficiencies of between two-thirds to three-quarters can be expected. There are also limitations with storage capacity and site locations.

An alternative to standby generation can in part be provided from interconnection with other continental utilities and demand management. The former already exists with a 2GW connection to France and a 500MW link to Northern Ireland. A 1.3GW link to the Netherlands is planned for 2010 with other projects under study. This would create a one-way dependency upon the continental system, already under resourced with transmission capacity and subject to significant intermittence from its own wind resource. With alternative use for trading, additional interconnection could present an attractive commercial option although not without strategic implications.

The position with demand management is not straightforward. This option is already adopted for large-scale industrial consumers. With domestic and commercial use, as an extension of system balancing, dedicated circuits are required whose installation and tariff would be through distribution utilities. The commercial viability with such schemes would be subject to inducement by tariff discount from normal usage. In addition the demand relief would be variable throughout the year and insignificant over the summer months. At best it could only complement other standby facilities. This option could create an opportunity for social subsidy but only if used as a last resort mechanism with an entire metered source affected. Normal use with dedicated circuits would realistically become a long-term project confined to new installation. The suggestion of refrigeration becoming an interruptible demand source would constrain operational effectiveness for system balancing.

It is crucial for the stability of the Grid system that means to cope with intermittency are fully robust. Comparison can be made with the scale of demand excursion being successfully accommodated; this assumes similar events from intermittence would also be satisfactorily managed. Such an assumption would be false as the natures of both requirements are different. Significant demand excursions are invariably predictable in scale and timing, intermittence events much less so with the added complication they can move in either direction. This prevents any anticipatory action with slower moving generation plant. Once pumped storage reserves are committed, response capability with remaining reserve is less certain and subject to time delay.

Robust dispatch is not confined to the response capability of generation plant but extends to the chain of command and control apparatus between control rooms. This comprises links for communication, computerised displays known as SCADA, printers and telephone contact, all supported by uninterruptible power supplies. The reliability of such equipment is an essential part of the whole chain of circumstance to receive information and implement instructions where widespread communication links are integral to the whole process. Although back-up systems are commonplace, the sheer scale and complexity of equipment involved cannot remove the risk, however unlikely, of interruption.

Fluctuating demand has always existed but largely confined to certain periods of the daily cycle. The introduction of intermittent generation (certainly with the scale projected) will present a continually changing scenario demanding constant corrective response. This circumstance violates a basic precept of sound operation that is to manage the Grid system with minimum adjustment. The exposure to interruption is far greater where timing of an incident can become the arbiter of system failure.

Further concern with Grid instability arises from Government attempts to remove obstacles in the way of promoting new renewable capacity to meet their targets. Transmission is currently seen to be a major constraint but the measures being proposed through the Transmission Access Review consultation, to remove these necessary and time worn practices, only erode the margin for error. With rising levels of intermittence into a dynamic, inherently unstable, unforgiving Grid system, such interference is manifestly unwise and requires experienced assessment.

The underlying need to cope with abnormal fluctuations of wind resource should define the extent such resource can be introduced. Given the accelerating pace of development, the sudden realisation of unacceptable instability would present a serious log jam of capacity with serious compensation implications. This scenario is more than possible within the restricted and exposed GB Grid system to Atlantic weather systems. In the absence of any overall responsibility for system performance and the negative consequences for participants to give any warning, unless definitive, a credible circumstance of failure exists, especially with such a high level of targeted wind resource. Existing assurances of technical adaptability contain caveats with implied open-ended cost resources and fragmented responsibility.

Sympathetic Tripping

Low rated generation is susceptible to tripping with any severe system disturbance caused by large generation loss or transmission fault. This effect in Germany led to the proportion of running standby generation, as a percentage of 7GW of installed wind capacity, being raised from 60% to 90%. As for the UK, recent Grid Codes have introduced stringent requirements to avert this condition but the scale of derogation from existing wind investment, the consistency of corrective measures, from wind farms within varied distribution utilities, all providing most new connection, raise doubts whether this problem can be sufficiently controlled.

National Grid presented an indication of this problem in their Incident Report into the widespread disconnection of consumers on 27 May 2008. 250MW of low rated generation plant appears to have been disconnected by this incident but it is not clear just how much plant was disconnected and whether this could ever be determined, such are the logistical realities. Only 580MW of demand was shed with low frequency relays when 1700MW might have been expected. Since privatisation the operational role of National Grid has been limited to providing balancing services with no overall responsibility for direct control, policing and performance. This extends to generation provision where reliance is placed upon the market for adjustment. This policy approach has resulted in a dangerous imbalance of generation mix, compounded by regulation and subsidy, constraining more economic options. Further confusion arises with wholly arbitrary renewable targets, supported by significant subsidy.

This Incident Report also provides evidence that should discourage the adoption of micro-generation. Perversely this is being encouraged by direct subsidy. With any scale of investment, the onset of a severe system disturbance would magnify the problems attending any incident. The report also reveals the absence of direct monitoring for generation embedded into distribution networks. This anomaly was a principal recommendation of a report into the widespread disconnection of supply across Europe in November 2006. The scale of wind resource to be accommodated on the GB grid system would require a fundamental review of arrangements monitoring connection, output and control across both grid and distribution connected generation. Currently only a limited proportion of grid connected wind capacity, confined to Scotland, is monitored for output, with no means of direct control.

The most revealing omission in this report by National Grid was the failure to address a number of issues of public concern, primarily the role of wind intermittency with this incident. This exposes the limited role of National Grid for their present responsibilities. Quite clearly there is no overview in place, no monitoring or policing and no authority being exercised over the GB Grid system across corporate interfaces.

The manifestation of these inadequacies is shown by the degree of failure to profit from measures sourced from continental experience.

Governor Response

The first line of correction with any variation of system frequency is governor response. This is an installed automatic feature with all synchronous generation plant that enables a limited correction to be given for restoration of frequency and is a continuous facility. Historically wind turbines have lacked this capability and although recent Grid Code changes have required this facility to be provided, it is not at all clear when or if it is being implemented. The extent of derogation with both grid and distribution connected wind turbines is uncertain. It is highly significant that within the UK there is no programme to replace wind turbines, unlike Germany where an estimated fifth of capacity is to be replaced.

The absence of this facility has a proportionate effect with frequency response variations and as nuclear generation governor response is normally limited for reasons of fuel economy, immediate relief to correct frequency deviation is denied. At periods of summer demand with wind turbulence, control of system frequency would become extremely difficult to manage.

Reactive Control

Coincident with establishing Grid Code modifications for governor response on wind turbines, corresponding measures for voltage control were introduced. Similar concerns arise with derogation and performance when large numbers are connected to areas of the network without any embedded demand. Failures to maintain correct voltage profiles are a source of instability and disconnection. Fluctuating output from wind resource also induce a higher incidence of transformer tap changing routines requiring more intensive maintenance scheduling. The final UCTE report from the continental incident of November 2006 also recommended the requirements for frequency and voltage variations of generation units connected to the distribution grid to be the same in terms of behaviour as that of units connected to the transmission network, becoming retrospective.

Technical Issues with Economic Implications

Standby Generation Investment
The circumstance of intermittency attending most renewable resource demands an almost similar capacity for standby generation with an appropriate response capability. The investment criteria for providing such capacity would demand sufficient load factor running to recoup this investment. With any scale of renewable resource, the opportunity for running would be restricted, thereby some method of alternative funding becomes necessary. Inevitably this would ultimately fall upon the consumer as a hidden subsidy.

Fuel Inefficiency with Standby Operation
Intermittent resource requires running standby generation to be available. With coal generation, minimum running is usually a quarter of full load representing two-thirds fuel efficiency in operation. Similar considerations apply to combined cycle gas turbine (CCGT) generation when part loaded but with less flexibility in operation.

Constrained-off payments
With any suggestion of conditions arising that could lead to Grid instability, recourse to constraining off generation capacity is implemented. Such measures provide high rewards to generation suppliers and provide the economic justification for new transmission investment decisions; all these additional costs are ultimately born by the consumer.

Reduced Load Factor with Wind Resource

Initial load factor estimates for GB wind resource had suggested a value of 35%. Calculations taken from Ofgem Renewable Obligation returns over a five-year period now indicate a reduced value of 25-26%. This represents an energy return 70% of the original estimate. A further consequence is the proportion of installed capacity that could be considered firm, reducing to 8% from 20%. This difference of installed capacity must be met from alternative generation investment in order to satisfy winter peak demand requirements for the Grid system.

Issues arising from 30GW of Wind Resource

There are several issues that arise from this intent to construct over 30GW of intermittent wind resource:

A. Generation dispersal would radically change the existing Grid system that is estimated by Ofgem to cost £10 billion.

B. A significant investment into fast response generation, interconnection facility or demand management would be needed as a standby provision.

C. This level of intermittent generation in conjunction with a necessary nuclear programme creates serious concerns for system stability with the restricted GB Grid system, particularly over the summer period. There would be persistent events when substantial generation capacity would need to be constrained off.

D. The scale of subsidy to be funded by the consumer combined with new transmission investment, additional standby generation provision, constrained off payment and inefficient Grid System operation, inevitably force an increasing proportion of consumers into fuel poverty.

E. The scale of cumulative cost arising with the above necessary accommodation would dwarf the original subsidy component, originally introduced to encourage renewable development. This subsidy is now being used for a mature technology.

F.   The manufacturing resources and expertise required for this investment would be located overseas.

Conclusion

To meet treaty requirements, logical analysis would prioritise conservation measures across all energy sectors without focussing upon electricity supply. There is a gross misapplication of resources into highly dubious, technically unsustainable and uneconomic renewable development. This is being sustained by pressure from commercial interests with short-term profit perspective.

The critical issue facing electricity supply is to restore an appropriate generation mix. Coal fired generation has to become a priority regardless of carbon sequestration. If state regulation insists on this facility, the State should become responsible for its provision. Germany already has in place a substantial new build programme for coal-fired generation, quite apart from the astonishing capacity being introduced in China and India. A combination of ageing plant and regulation is forcing generation capacity in the UK to be retired from service, well before any nuclear capacity could come on stream. Measures now being taken to introduce a nuclear programme are a decade too late, at the price of having lost indigenous capability and with inflated cost. The failure to continue nuclear construction after Sizewell was a monumental mistake. Promoting intermittent uneconomic renewable capacity with supporting uneconomic standby plant is absurd. A pre-occupation with targets, misplaced subsidy and regulation has distorted economic choices for achieving an imposed EU objective.

Derek G Birkett
11 September 2008

APPENDIX 5C

COMMENT ON CONSERVATIVE GREEN POLICY DOCUMENT NO 8

The Low Carbon Economy

Background I am a chartered electrical engineer with a lifetime working within the electrical supply industry and have been a party member for over twenty five years. This experience has seen operational duties with coal and hydro generation, power station construction at five locations, including three nuclear, on installation and commissioning and for twenty years undertaking shift duties on grid system control in the North of Scotland.

Overview A fundamental premise to the paper is the requirement to 'go green' regardless of the economic and technical realities involved. Energy is the keystone of advanced economies where the cost, rather than its provision, is the deciding factor promoting economic growth. Electricity has the advantage of being obtained from a variety of energy sources but disadvantage with its inability to be stored, at least in any significant quantity. It must be produced as needed, in a virtually instant timescale, making its supply highly vulnerable to disruption. The choice of fuel source should not be restricted in any sense, if the lowest market value is to be realised. While strategic imperatives are bound to conflict with this ideal, the fundamental question remains as to who should decide the manner and scale of this interference into a free market. Inevitably the State assumes this role with its resources of knowledge and responsibility for national security, at least in an historical sense. However we now have a system of political control where diffusion of responsibility is widespread and where energy is being used as a political tool. Far-reaching and fundamental decisions are being made at an international level, where conflict has become confined to economic exploitation as opposed to territorial acquisition, the latter now demanding disproportionate resources. Private capital has accumulated on a scale exceeding the resources of most nation states, with all the consequent influence within national and global politics.

Introduction It is self evident that the paper has been produced without any professional scientific or technical advice. This deficiency is so extensive that it would be tedious to explain the numerous inconsistencies. What is obvious is the determined attempt to create and sustain financial frameworks that can exploit the myopic political decision to combat climate change by diktat. This not only restricts economic choice for generation but also introduces such extensive subsidy as to cripple operation of the normal market for electrical supply.

Energy Policy The paper is right to encourage nuclear development but in opposition the Party has failed miserably to promote the obvious need for such technology. The failure to promote nuclear construction after Sizewell has condemned an indigenous industry to oblivion. Its record of silence when Westinghouse was sold, a matter of months before change in Government policy, only revealed the inadequacy and lack of foresight with its existing policy. For a whole decade, Government policy had been for renewable development, yet the dangers were not foreseen or opposed with the consequence we now have a dangerously imbalanced generation portfolio that will take decades to put right. Again the failure to foresee the consequences arising from changes to the Pool market for generation payment, underlines this miserable record. Given the public mood, these deficiencies were no doubt prompted by expediency, rather than informed conviction.

What is encouraging in the paper is the (essential) need for coal-fired generation to be adopted (and as a matter of urgency) where existing coal capacity is rapidly ageing. The technical need has not been fully grasped as it provides the most effective means to cope with increasing demand fluctuation brought on by renewable (wind) development. The requirement for sequestration, as you indicate, should be a matter for the state. This is essential to progress construction. The concept of sequestration, given its scale, can only be a fig leaf in the present circumstances.

The whole concept of micro-generation is flawed and would introduce a series of technical complications and ultimately consumer resentment. Current experience has been a failure and to continue would only reveal the Party to have learnt nothing. The cost of specialist attendance does not warrant the suggested gain, especially when the scheme would be subsidised with no certainty of extended life. The public by now is well aware of the 'derivative' culture bringing us all into such a sorry mess and these suggested schemes have such an imprint.

The portrayal of outdated grid technology is simply absurd and the promotion of 'smart metering' misplaced. Its effect would be marginal at best in any domestic location and confidence with variable costing would soon evaporate where the opportunity for dispute is so reliant on the technology, particularly when imposed. Again consumer resentment should become a very real consideration. The suggestion of its use in domestic circumstance to create negative demand for system balancing is impractical. Necessary modification would be confined to new installation and the supplier would need recompense from the National Grid. Further its contribution in summer would be negligible.

What these suggestions reveal is an insidious attempt to gain commercial benefit at consumer expense. A bandwagon introduced when the Renewable Obligation was introduced. This contagion affects all utilities, including transmission and explains the commercial enthusiasm for renewable development in Scotland where transmission constraints are such as to present a considerable bonus for utilities with constrained off payments, above the very generous terms of subsidy. The agenda of the Scottish Government in promoting renewable development is to become ingratiated with the EU in their drive for independence, regardless of the financial and environmental cost inflicted.

The item of most concern within this paper is the continuation of existing renewable policy that I know to be unsustainable for the GB Grid system. The suggestion that the intended scale of intermittency can be managed by negative demand and interconnection is deeply flawed and the evidence presented at the recent House of Lords hearing on renewable energy, makes the point that virtually all renewable capacity must be replicated by conventional means. When all this generating capacity is added to the pressing need to replace ageing nuclear and coal capacity with regulatory withdrawal over this next decade, before new nuclear capacity comes on stream, the question must be asked as to where the resources, financial, technical and manufacturing, are to come from and at what cost. All this in a competing international market where our own manufacturing and technical resources have become so denuded.

Reference has been made to interconnection (at no small cost) and this is largely induced by renewable development. There is a political dimension to this investment; such connection would become essential for Grid system security but it would become a one-way dependence, as the continental Grid is seven times the size of our own. Currency independence becomes meaningless when our power structure is so beholden.

Conclusion. It must be obvious that over time, all these realities and abuses will become known and public reaction faced. When combined with increasing scepticism over man-made global warming, fuel poverty and the looming insecurity and cost of power supplies, the political reaction will be devastating. It is the duty of opposition to spell out this circumstance now, if any credibility is to remain when this reaction comes. This paper utterly fails to address this inevitable scenario that would in all likelihood have to be faced by the Party when in Government.

Derek G Birkett   8 February 2009

APPENDIX 5D

National Grid Consultation –

SUBMISSION BY DEREK G BIRKETT

Background Experience
The author is a retired Grid control engineer having twenty years of operational experience controlling the Electricity Grid in the North of Scotland. Prior to joining system control, several years of experience with the operation of hydro and coal fired generating plant were acquired, all on shift duties. Related experience over a decade on project work was obtained with installation and commissioning at five power stations, three of which were Nuclear, as an employee of the CEGB and TNPG, attaining section engineer status. A degree in electrical engineering from Leeds University led to the award of Chartered Engineer with this project involvement.

Introduction
The productive absorption of intermittent renewable energy on the GB Grid system is a technical issue where expertise in confined to a few score of individuals. This agenda has been forced on the industry by political pressure against all economic criteria and without technical guidance. The scale of subsidy introduced by Government policy has created extensive distortions into a market where commercial and political considerations override technical good sense. The issue in hand is how to accommodate the scale of intermittency with renewable generation without compromising system security.

Basic Principles

A glance at first principles would not be out of place. Predictable generation has always been the foundation of ensuring system stability. The time-worn principle not to encourage uncontrollable generation has been jettisoned. The consequence of renewable investment is increased volatility, flouting the principle of minimum adjustment to ensure smooth running of the Grid system. Already on average, almost fifty loading adjustments each hour are exercised for system balancing alone with all the consequential cost of maintenance, plant deterioration and reliability. With increasing renewable investment, these adjustments would not be linear but exponential in character forcing a retrograde 'fly by wire' or automatic system of control to be implemented. Once introduced the manual system would rapidly degrade, creating reliance on automation with profound implications for fault retrieval situations and back up reliability. The consequence would be further exposure to risk.

Certain techniques could avoid this unwanted measure. Renewable tidal energy with its predictable cycle is a promising technology but demands disciplined exploitation. A combination of the various technologies could be dovetailed to eventually create a constant generation output throughout the twenty-four hour cycle enabling a stand-alone facility that could be largely independent of the plant scheduling process. A similar approach across the border interconnection to Scotland would maintain constant power transfer by combining wind, hydro and pumped storage into a combined generation mix. Another technique would be to reinstate a merit order of generation based upon plant response and running costs and not on market price signals. Increasingly it is the response capability of the balancing source becoming the critical determinant. Currently the market tail wags the generation dog. Such new thinking has to come before automated response.

Minds should concentrate on the effects of system failure that while currently statistically insignificant, when they do occur have devastating impact. There is a human factor with exhaustion or pandemic with irreplaceable specialist staff. The extended loss of power supply to a major city has consequences far beyond any narrow commercial consideration. I am reminded of the final report into the system incident of 27 May 2008 when no recommendation was made to increase response and reserve levels, based on the economic case with clause 6.5. The cost to the consumer was utterly ignored. There is an ethical dimension lacking, all too prominent with the recent turmoil in financial markets.

Generation Scheduling

The principal scheduling challenge to accommodate both fluctuating demand and wind resource is to have sufficient response capability available to overcome the most extreme fluctuations that could be anticipated. Forecasting has limited application, as contingency is the necessary requirement. Sufficient experience of wind fluctuation can be accessed from continental experience with allowance being made for Atlantic exposure. A good example came on 29 October 2000 in Denmark when a 41% swing with an installed wind capacity of almost 2GW arose within an hour.

The system is most at risk when unexpected events coincide, often prompted by severe weather conditions. This is not confined to transmission trips or generator loss but also communication and equipment failure. In the past the latter events, though rare, were often ridden through, being at times of relative inactivity that existed throughout most of the twenty-four hour period. This circumstance no longer holds and increasingly loading or balancing adjustments have become a continual and intense activity. Recourse to statistical techniques to determine probability of events often belies the operational reality of having to keep some contingency reserve, not simply as a 'just in case' scenario but the consequential awareness for any remote risk of failure. Sophisticated modelling aids have to accommodate the bigger picture. All too easily such aids can become an operational constraint.

With loading response, comparison is often made between meeting system demand excursions and wind volatility to justify system accommodation. The nature of response with both cases is quite different. Predominately demand excursions can be predicted with some degree of accuracy based upon past experience. This is not true with wind volatility as events are much less predictable, more frequent with scale unknown and crucially the direction of movement uncertain. This last characteristic prevents anticipatory loading that is a crucial component with any loading response to a demand excursion.

Mitigating Intermittency

As an independent witness at the Beauly-Denny Public Inquiry, a personal judgement was given with the level of wind resource on the GB Grid system at which severe problems of stability would become evident. This equated to the then current operational and consented wind capacity of around 6GW. This estimate is to some degree elastic and dependent upon the scale of investment allocated to the problem. Mitigation would primarily come from interconnection with other grid systems and additional pumped storage capacity. The former would have a political dimension as it could create a circumstance of one-way dependency upon the Continental Grid system while with the latter, surprise is expressed for not being advocated within the 'gone green' 2020 scenario. Recent intent of SSE to invest into further pumped storage capacity within the Highland region is entirely predictable.

Alternative means to mitigate intermittency are outlined in your consultation document. Scale and cost become prime determinants and are advocated as commercial alternatives. I would hope wider counsel might prevail.To chart a path with so many variables and uncertainties with system security, making refrigeration a tool for demand control, is to become hostage to fortune with excessive use and risk with indeterminate food quality deterioration. Likewise with electric car transportation where cost and risk is borne by the customer. The imposition of 'smart' metering for the domestic scene is more about access to meter reading (and remote disconnection?) than customer information and is not without considerable social implications. Once novelty wore off, habits of domestic routine would be re-imposed. The cost of modification (who would pay?) for dedicated circuits would confine such use to new installation, becoming a facility only in the long term. Another consideration is seasonal response from heating load where summer relief is almost non-existent. My view is that such techniques in the domestic sphere would provide very limited scope for system balancing unless heavily subsidised or subject to regulation.

The concept of variable costing (except for white meter) would be open to error and abuse without effective means of correlation from the consumer end. Would a third category of white meter control for the daily peak demand period not provide a more common sense solution for domestic customers with colour code identification for metering?

I would view micro-generation on any scale with some concern having maverick effects with system faults and disturbances. It is not at all clear how this problem can be overcome without excessive and costly precaution. As with any new regulation, the time lag with full implementation considering scale, dispersion and derogation may last for years and without effective policing could never be achieved. The logistical and bureaucratic challenge would be considerable. The proposals of the Conservative party on micro-generation are seen as little more than commercial opportunism. The general public seldom factors specialist maintenance and repair costs into the viability of micro-generation. Heat pumps would appear to offer the best option for development but with limited scope for most domestic situations. Back feed tariffs do not entice.

A versatile means of managing intermittency is found with coal-fired generation that is expected to reduce significantly with the 'Gone Green' scenario and is a major economic casualty with Government policy. From a strategic perspective it is incomprehensible with having a secure fuel supply at home and abroad, reducing reliance upon CCGT generation and denying fuel option, so important with market pricing.

Of all forms of generation, conventional hydro has the most favourable characteristics and provides the most rapid rate of response even when idle. Although renewable, being capital intensive has deterred its exploitation yet an estimated 0.5GW of further large hydro (with storage) could be constructed with any long-term perspective. The low availability statistic of 60% as given in para 6.55 is grossly misleading. This derives from its annual load factor with run-off and de-rating of certain plant in cascade to qualify for ROC payment. Reliability is exceptional and storage enables flexible regimes of operation throughout the year, if exercised in moderation. It has potential for system balancing with fluctuating capacity available when day before notice is given.

Embedded Generation

The proliferation of wind resource as dispersed embedded generation on the scale being promoted has many concerns. These issues come to light with the report on the 27 May 2008 Grid incident where the scale and content with discrepancies between the preliminary and final reports suggest an emasculated role of National Grid to monitor real time events than previously. Comment on the preliminary report is made as an appendix, leaving many questions unanswered within the final report. Predominant is the role of embedded wind generation to influence the third drop in frequency, leading to low frequency relay disconnection of consumers. The explanation discounting this effect is unconvincing. A related issue is the apparent lack of support from the Dinorwic pumped storage facility for this incident. This drives the need for further pumped storage capacity to avoid the dependence upon a single dominant station location that is independent of the cross border interconnection to Scotland with its stability constraint.

A problem touched on previously is the scale of derogation and observance of Grid Code compliance with the extent of dispersed wind generation plant through a multitude of DNOs with no direct incentive to comply. This is compounded with wind farms in England not being subject to the Grid Codes below 50MW capacity. Policing of developers seems to be confined to the time of commissioning. What incentive is there to comply and what penalty exists for non-observance? The extensive replacement programme of wind turbines in Germany provides ample opportunities for secondary deployment within the UK. Just how extensive is the derogation for existing wind turbines on the GB Grid system?

A major recommendation by the UCTE following the continental grid incident of November 2006 was that all distribution connected generation should have the same behaviour during frequency and voltage variations as for units connected to the transmission network, becoming retrospective. In addition system operators are to receive on-line data of distribution connected generation. These conditions are not applied across the GB power network system; the monitoring of wind output for England and Wales to the system operator with onshore wind is not evident. Future proposals and organisation with offshore development should introduce a much-improved rigour for Grid Code compliance.

The scale of wind resource proposed introduces much greater risk for system splits to arise, particularly from Scotland. To enable reconnection in manageable timescales, volatility with frequency would become a serious problem. To disable grid connected wind farms in a controlled manner over forty-five minutes still leaves embedded generation. In storm conditions such volatility would become extreme. How is this to be managed, raising the prospect of pre-empting the problem in extreme weather conditions by shutdown at considerable cost. In practice the problem and risk would no doubt be endured.

Stability of remote wind resource

Transmission design assumptions for wind resource give a dispersion factor of 60%. Coupled with proposals to share capacity for low load factor generation, reduced risk of trip criteria and the premature connection with 450MW of Highland wind capacity, these items would introduce constraints with summer gale conditions. Intertrip schemes may well be deployed. Performance with voltage regulation (and uniform frequency response) with any scale of wind resource may be problematic in areas with little consumer demand as anchor and derogated capacity. The technology is quite recent and unproven on this scale. This circumstance is rapidly evolving and therefore prone to the unexpected. The issue of uniform frequency response and voltage regulation for wind turbines seems to be a critical determinant for National Grid in accepting the scale of wind resource proposed where reliance on conditions contained in paras 5.21 and 5.24 would be critical.

Transmission

The ambitious proposals contained in the recent ENSG document have assumed an unlimited absorption of over 30GW from wind resource. Has any recognition been taken for contingency planning if this target, for whatever reason, were not found to be feasible? A good example arises with the Beauly/Denny project that is not required for 2020 renewable targets. Its construction would allow wind farm development across the southern Highlands thereby desecrating the landscape that supports tourism. An east coast alternative is available with upgrading that would ultimately constitute part of the final transmission scheme post 2020. The capability of this line cannot be realised until the restriction with the border interconnection is resolved. This interconnection has a far greater priority for any GB System upgrading and is a prime source of excessive constrained off payments. This item is the tip of a very large iceberg. Are the investigations with SQSS standards in para 4.40 to accommodate 1800MW disconnection intended to cover Scotland?

Reliability of Generation and Estimates

As already stated, response capability would become a critical issue for accommodating intermittency. There are several developing constraints:

*   The retirement of plant with the LCPD regulation.
*   The increasing age and reduced reliability with fossil plant.
*   The increasing predominance of CCGT generation for responsive use. This has exposure to type faults, gas supply constraints and reduced on line flexibility.
*   Reduced nuclear contribution with declining reliability.
*   Increasing operational activity reducing overall long-term reliability.

The current estimate of 3% for managing residual demand can be expected to become much larger (as recognised) from increasing levels of micro-generation and embedded generation with significant implications for control techniques.

Availability of Resources

As a consequence of inadequate Government policy over the past two decades the current mix of generation plant is seriously out of balance to accommodate construction timescales, an ageing profile and resilience against cost fluctuations. This has coincided with a policy of uneconomic renewable development, primarily that of wind resource that is 'additional to', not 'replacement for' (HofL Renewable Inquiry) the necessary investment with fully controllable conventional generation plant, all having their individual range of complementary characteristics. This scale of necessary replacement is without precedent, compounded by regulation that constrains economic choice. Together with constructional programmes throughout Europe, competition for resources of capital, manufacturing and technical skills are expected to be strong in a seller's market. This at a time when credit is restricted, the manufacturing base in the UK has shrunk and apprentice training neglected. With nuclear construction considered as an important component of this essential commitment, substantial investment over most of a decade will be necessary before any energy is produced. Overall this circumstance is a recipe for project delays and cost overruns. In terms of energy supply and economics, logic would question the role for renewable investment, particularly when it undermines the economic case for new conventional standby plant. Insufficient margin with total generation capacity only compounds the increasing problems in handling intermittency. The gravity of this whole situation is not being adequately addressed.

Information Transparency

Historically National Grid had claimed a 35% load factor for GB wind resource that with recent analysis from Ofgem ROC returns now indicate a value of around 26% (the Gone Green scenario has assumed 35%). Allowing for significant offshore development, current estimates now promote 30% load factor that seems optimistic. These figures are of far reaching consequence with the initial justification for investment and planning approval, return on investment, establishing a capacity credit to offset against system peak generation requirements and not least the eventual plant capacity required to meet EU and UK renewable targets.

Further transparency is needed to reveal costs to the customer of not only the Renewable Obligation subsidy needed to promote expansion, representing a fraction of the overall cost from having a renewable agenda, but related expense with investment into transmission connection and reinforcement, system balancing needs, standby plant incentive and constrained off payments to generators as compensation for transmission restrictions.

Cost estimates in the past have not inspired confidence and cannot be relied upon, in particular when a specific agenda is being promoted. Without such information the full consequences of energy policy cannot be evaluated as a basis for change. In the long term no policy is immutable.

Conclusion

The combination of technical change, uncertainties, developing constraints and necessary scale of generation replacement, coincident with having to manage increasing intermittency, presents a scenario of unacceptable hazard. When set against the consequence of failure, any assessment of risk should adopt a cautionary principle. With decades of past system stability taken for granted, this departure from sound practice, driven in a climate of excessive subsidy, haste and recession, presents a test of nerve where no clear overriding technical authority exists. The circumstance for commercial gain is evident, institutional pressure must be intense.

Any historical perspective would question the imperative of man-made climate change with so much scientific dissent when the premium is so ruinous and potentially destructive. Reduction of carbon emissions from renewable generation when placed into global perspective has limited effect when set against deforestation and energy savings. The need for energy security by becoming less dependent on imported energy is more persuasive but the means chosen would integrate this goal into a European entity while enfeebling national economic strength to influence events within that entity.

This judgement of unacceptable hazard comes from a background of twenty years' experience with direct operational system control, the behaviour of frequency conditions being a constant reference with all loading instructions. The imperative of maintaining system balance is evident but the vulnerabilities and risks are not. This cavalier approach in dismissing operational knowledge for institutional gain will bear heavily in years to come. Such frankness as explained can only come from a retired position.

Derek G Birkett
24 July 2009

Appendix. Observations with the National Grid Investigation into disconnection on 27 May 2008 (dated 28 July 2008).

Index

Hairy Mole's

Adventures

on the

High Seas

by

Chris Owen

Rans🐾m

Hairy Mole's Adventures on the High Seas

by Chris Owen
Illustrated by David Mostyn

Published by Ransom Publishing Ltd.
Radley House, 8 St. Cross Road, Winchester,
Hampshire SO23 9HX
www.ransom.co.uk

ISBN   978 184167 083 6

First published in 2007
This edition published 2013

A CIP catalogue record of this book is available from the British Library.

Dedications

I would like to dedicate this book to Dylan Ford, Jack Seddon, all the little Dennisons, Amelie Furniss, Rose and Arthur Lazarus, Sheldon and Savannah Harrison, Benson Mariner, Chioddi and Shania Smith, and Amy Wood.

Remember you are the future - don't mess it up!

Special thanks to all the good people I met at Camping Girasole in Tuscany, Italy, especially all the pirates.

Final thanks to Nikki Cheal for being lovely and very understanding.

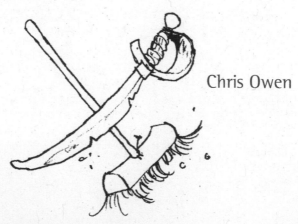

Chris Owen

Chapter One

Contemplation

Hairy Mole sat on the side of the concrete jetty and flared his huge nostrils at the sea.

He could smell the Seven Sizzling Sausages that were being prepared for his breakfast;

he could smell the gentle breeze that contained just a hint of lemon washing powder and more than a suggestion of freshly cut grass from Mr Bernard's wide and varied garden.

But, most of all, do you know what Hairy Mole could smell? Hairy Mole could smell the salt of the sea, he could smell the fishing nets and he could smell the tarpaulin used to cover the little boats as they bobbed up and down, up and down, at the side of the concrete jetty.

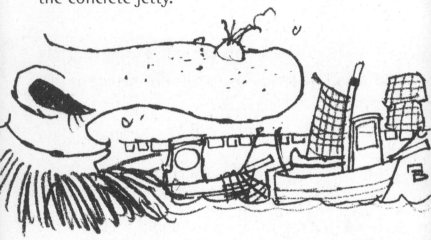

As Hairy Mole sniffed and breathed in all the smells of the sea, his mind, once again, turned to adventure. However, there was still the matter of Seven Sizzling Sausages to deal with, so Hairy Mole got to his feet and headed for his mother's kitchen.

Mrs Bulbous Mole was content with her life. She had accomplished everything she wanted to do and now she was happy to see the ^{su}n in the morning and to watch the $_st_ar_s$ in the evening.

If it was too cloudy for ^{su}n or $_st_ar_s$ Mrs Bulbous Mole was still happy,

as she knew that they would be out the next day

and this was something to look forward to.

Mrs Mole was also very proud of her son. Hairy knew that he wanted to be a pirate and even though he only had a little ship and a small crew of $^{rag}-_{tag}$ urchins, he followed his heart and tried the best he could.

Bulbous was very proud indeed and she smiled to herself as she turned the Seven Si^z$_z$ling SausageS over in the pan.

Hairy Mole stood in the kitchen doorway, hands on hips, hairs in nostrils and itch on bottom. After a quick s^{c}r$_a^{t}_c$h Hairy Mole announced his intentions:

"Mother, 1 am to set off, once again, to discover new lands, high adventure, possible treasure and definite jam."

"My boy, 1 am proud! Now come and eat your Seven Si^z$_z$ling SausageS before they lose their Si^z$_z$le."

10

Mrs Mole busied herself setting the plate on the table while her son continued:

"I have the whiff of the sea in my nostrils and the scent of care-free spirit in my cheeks!" Hairy Mole declared, finally sitting down at the wooden kitchen table.

Bulbous Mole grimaced at the prospect of any kind of scent appearing from between her son's cheeks, but smiled happily at his passion as he tucked into his breakfast.

Chapter Two

A Pirate Hunt

Hairy Mole left his mother's house with a full belly and a shiny new belt.

He had other pirate clothes too, but the belt was

ever so shiny

so it deserved a special mention, particularly as his other pirate clothes were looking slightly worn and patchy,

especially around the pit areas.

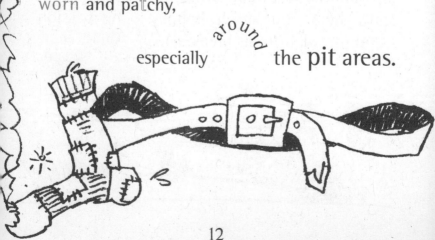

Hairy Mole planned to sail the <u>very next</u> <u>day</u>, and so needed to gather his crew from whatever pirate activities they were currently involved in.

First he tried the boat yard, as he knew Mr Barnacle often hired pirates to clean the seaweed from his fishing boats.

Sure enough, under a seaweed-covered boat, there appeared a gigantic pair of feet. The toes wiggled and stretched as if they had a mind of their own.

The feet were ever so smelly and Hairy Mole knew that they could only belong to one particular person. Hairy Mole pinched the largest, most disgusting toe and waited for the rest of the body to appear.

"Oi Oi! What's the bother, Mr Barnacle? I be pickin' as quick as I can!"

Pickle the Pirate sat straight upright, squinting in the sunshine to see who was making mischief with one of his ten tooters.

"Hairy Mole, it's you! I'll get my baggage."

With that, Pickle was on his feet and, after a bit of playful wrestling, they arranged to meet by Hairy Mole's little ship at 7 a m s h a r p the next morning.

The next members of the crew were found at the Post Office. Crevice and Pit, the twins, were very useful post sorters, what with their eye for detail and their extra-large hands.

The twins were more than happy to abandon the mail for the promise of possible treasure and <u>definite</u> jam.

"Count us in Hairy Mole, 7am tomorrow, sharp!"

Crevice and Pit both shouted together as they threw the post

into the air,

much to Postmaster Will's obvious horror.

Next, to the pub, but not for boozin' mind!

Hairy Mole knew his crew well enough to know where to find them. B e l c h had spent the last few days in the pub cellar using his giant nose to aid Mr Lockley the Innkeeper.

Mr Lockley had lost all his labels for the beer and had managed to muddle up all the pipes, so no one knew what was going where.

Belch had been sniffing at the barrels trying to work out what was Ale and what was Pale.

To be honest, Belch looked as though he had been more than sniffing the barrels, as

Hairy Mole

found him

st^agg^{er}ing

up

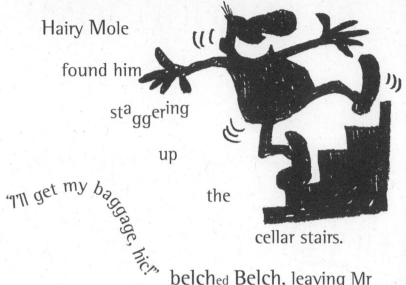

the

cellar stairs.

"I'll get my baggage, hic!"

belch_{ed} **Belch**, leaving Mr Lockley scrat_{ch}ing his head at the empty barrels in the cellar.

"7 a^m s h^a _rp tomorrow, count me in.

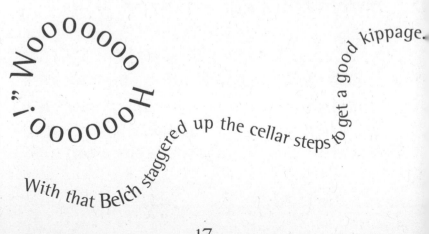

"Wooooooooo

Hooooooo!"

With that Belch staggered up the cellar steps to get a good kippage.

Suddenly, there was an almighty

KABOOOOOOOM!

The old cobbled stones under Hairy Mole's feet shuddered and shook.

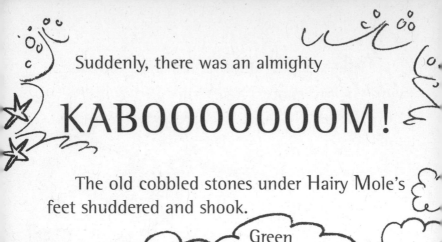

Green smoke billowed from a door along the street.

The smoke was quickly followed by a coughing and spluttering figure with big ears, burnt hair and covered in green slime.

A second figure appeared through the smoke, shoutin' and hollerin' at the first. Mrs Gumdrop, the sweet-shop owner, chased the green figure out on to the cobbled street, hitting her over the head with a cinnamon stick.

"That's the last time you and your ideas work in my shop. Never mix Dib-Dabs with Bon-Bons with Space Dust! Now off with you, urchin!"

With that the coughing figure ran to the waterside and lay on the floor, laughing at the sky.

Hairy Mole approached the chuckling, green urchin.

"7 am sharp tomorrow, Guff my girl," said Hairy Mole, stifling a laugh through his whiskers.

"I'll get my baggage!" trifled Guff.

Hairy Mole smiled to himself. His crew were almost together again.

There was **Pickle** with his extra-large feet,

Crevice and **Pit**, the twins, with their extra-large hands,

Belch, with his extra-big nose, and finally

Guff, with her large ears and big ideas.

Hairy Mole continued his walk through the little seaside village, turning corners and following winding passages until he came across the village green.

20

Stamp, knock. "Four!"

Hairy Mole stood for a while and listened.

Stamp, knock. "Four!"

There it was again, this time followed by a slight spluttering of applause, as if lots of people were clapping with only two fingers on each hand.

Stamp, knock. "Six! Woo hoo!" the voice squeaked in delight.

As Hairy Mole walked across the large village green he saw his old friend and first mate, Mr Bogey. Mr Bogey was standing in the middle of the green thwacking a red cricket ball as far as he could with his left leg. Mr Bogey had actually had his left leg replaced with a cricket bat after an incident in the West Indies, but he doesn't like to squeak - I mean speak - about it.

"Hairy Mole, I'm one hundred not out! This lot aren't a patch on the West Indians"
squeaked Mr Bogey in his ever so ^{high-pitched} voice.

"Well done, Green. 7 a^m tomorrow s ^ha _rp." Hairy Mole waved at Mr Bogey.

"I'll get my baggage after tea," squeaked a delighted First Mate Bogey.

Stamp, knock, and thwack. " _{Woo hoo!} " Another Bogey six sailed out of the village green.

So there they were, seven pirates to sail the seven seas with a breakfast of seven sizzling sausages inside the hairiest.

A job well done, thought Hairy Mole, as he returned to his little house to pack his own baggage ready for 7 _am _s ^ha _rp the next day.

Chapter Three

Don't Forget Your Baggage!

The very next day, at 7 a m   s h a r p, Hairy Mole stood on board his little ship. There were two sails and a cabin containing seven hammocks and a table for eating.

There isn't much more to say about the ship, except that it was little and had two sails and a cabin with seven hammocks and a table for eating - but I have said that already and promise I won't say it again!

Hairy Mole stood and watched. He watched the waves gently rocking the ship. He watched the seagulls, one of which looked vaguely familiar. But Hairy Mole mainly watched the gangplank and wondered who would be the first to arrive.

He watched the gangplank and waited and waited.

Stamp,
knock.

      Stamp,
      knock.

            Stamp,
            knock.

Guess who was first onto the gangplank at 7:00am sharp?

"Mr Bogey!" called down Hairy Mole. "How are your barnacles?"

"Hairy Mole!" squeaked up Mr Bogey. "How are your cockles?"

Mr Bogey and Hairy Mole gave each other manly pats on the back and stood together, watching and waiting.

The next two arrivals waved excitedly with their extremely large hands as they boarded the ship at 7:05am sharpish.

Can you guess who they were?

"Ah, the twins," bellowed Hairy Mole.

"Crevice and Pit, good to see you lads," squeaked Mr Bogey, knocking his cricket bat leg on the floor in delight: knock, knock, knock.

"Who's there?" asked Crevice and Pit together.

"Where can we unload our baggage? Where are we sleeping?" The twins looked at Hairy Mole for an answer.

"Pit,
first bunk on the left.   Crevice,
                            first bunk on the right."

Hairy Mole chuckled to himself as Crevice
and Pit raced down
                        the
                                stairs to find their
                                        sleeping quarters.

Hairy Mole turned his attention back to
the gangplank where he continued to wait,
occasionally tutting as he glanced at his Pirate's
Old-fashioned Pocket Watch.

The next to arrive bounded up the
gangplank as quickly as his two giant feet
would carry him. According to Hairy Mole's
Old-fashioned Pirate's Pocket Watch, the time
was 7.10am.

Not very s h a r p i s h !

Can you guess who these freakish feet belonged to? A clue – it's what you do to onions at Christmas time (poor things!).

"Pickle, you large-footed mutant, how are you my lad?" Hairy Mole welcomed Pickle onto the ship with more backslapping and friendly time-keeping tutting from Mr Bogey.

"I couldn't tie my laces, it takes so long don't you know!" laughed Pickle.

"Tell me about it some other time. Now, second on the left for you, off you go."

With that Pickle went to join Crevice and Pit down below in the sleeping quarters.

The time ticked by and before long it was 7.20am. Mr Bogey shook his head and glanced at his own Old-fashioned Pirate's Pocket Watch.

"These young 'uns could do with new alarm clocks, wouldn't you say, Hairy Mole?"

"They could do with new bones, Mr Bogey. The ones that they have appear to be too lazy!" grumbled Hairy Mole.

"I heard that!" came a voice from over the other side of the ship.

Now, who could have heard the two pirates from that far away? Only someone with ever such large ears!

"Guuuuuuuuuffff!" bellowed Hairy Mole.

"What time do you call this?" squeaked Mr Bogey, hands on hips, eyebrows standing to attention.

"I would say 7.20 am, decidedly un sharpish," mumbled Guff.

"I would agree. Now, off you go with your baggage, shipshape and second bunk on the right!" Guff shot straight down the stairs without another mumble.

Hairy Mole began to count on his warty fingers: "*One*, Hairy Mole,
    two, Mr Bogey,
      three, Pickle,
        four & *five*, Crevice & Pit,
          six, a tiny Guff
            and *seven*, *seven*, where is ... "

"Buuuuuuurp!" burped Belch, before Hairy Mole had a chance to finish.

"That will be seven pirates altogether then!" nodded Mr Bogey, as Belch made his way up the gangplank, looking slightly green and smelling slightly off.

"I pity your large nose, Belch, I really do!" tutted Hairy Mole.

"Am I third on the left or third on the right?" asked a tired-looking Belch.

"Third on the left, thank you. Now shipshape and ahoy to you," squeaked Mr Bogey.

"Way hey the anchor and up the riggers, me monkeys!" cried Hairy Mole with glee.

With that, the little pirate ship with two sails, seven hammocks and a table for eating left the harbour and started out on its new voyage.

Just as they were almost out of sight  of the harbour, a familiar cry was heard from up amongst the clouds.

It was Toby the Seagull.

"All together again?" squawked Toby.

"As I live and breath yes, and I have never felt so happy!" answered Hairy Mole, as he stood behind the wooden wheel at the front of the ship.

"Enjoy the moment, Hairy Mole, because sometimes it's better to look forward with happiness rather than when the moment is upon you, and you have no time to notice."

With that, Toby the Seagull flew *high* into the sky and squawked with laughter until he was out of sight and sound.

"That's easy for you to say, Mr Seagull," chuckled Hairy Mole to himself, as he steered the little ship to the horizon and out of sight of land.

Chapter Four

Where Are We Going?

The little ship bobbed on the ocean. Up and down, up and down went the waves. Up and down, up and down went the pirates.

Splosh and splash went the waves, as they splished and sploshed onto the little ship.

"Wooooo!" and *"Wheeey!"* cried the pirates, as they continued on their journey to the horizon and beyond.

Crevice and Pit worked hard with buckets to splash the sea back to where it had come from. Their extra-large hands made easy work of the job and it wasn't long before the little ship was sailing on calmer waters.

Hairy Mole was at the wheel with a map crumpled in front of him. His big, warty finger was pointing at a place on the map as Mr Bogey joined him.

"Ah-ha! First mate Bogey, there you are!" smiled Hairy Mole.

"Here I am!" squeaked Mr Bogey. "But where are we, Hairy Mole?"

Hairy Mole let out a pirate laugh that he had been practising for several weeks:

"Hoo hoo Haa haa Heeee heee!" laughed Hairy Mole.

"Pardon?" squeaked Mr Bogey.

"Hoo hoo Haa haa Heeeeee heeee!"
laughed Hairy Mole again. This time he held his big belly and leant his head back for full pirate laugh effect.

"Hairy Mole?" enquired Mr Bogey, as he wasn't quite sure if his friend was feeling quite himself.

"Come *hither* Mr Bogey, and look at my pirate map."

Hairy Mole held out the map for Mr Bogey to get a proper look.

"We are heading for a country in Europe where the cheese is called formaggio and the fine wine is called bueno vino!" Hairy Mole pointed at the map.

"Do they have eggs?" squeaked Mr Bogey, slightly concerned.

"They have chickens and they call them pollo, so they must have eggs," answered Hairy Mole, slightly concerned that Mr Bogey hadn't been impressed by his grasp of a foreign language.

"Do you want to know the name of this country, *or what?*" grumbled Hairy Mole.

"Well, OK then," squeaked Mr Bogey, slightly concerned at Hairy Mole's lack of thought for his favourite food.

"We are bound for Italy, or Italia as the Italians say. It is to the west of Greece and to the east of Spain and it is in the Mediterranean Sea. The people of Italy are very friendly and sing and dance all day, when they are not sleeping! There are untold beautiful treasures and the *finest* jam." Hairy Mole beamed at his bountiful knowledge of another country.

"I see!" squeaked Mr Bogey. "And are we almost in Italy then?" he asked.

"We will know when we see a flag with the colours green, white and red in 3 bold stripes."

Hairy Mole beamed again, thanking his lucky stars that he had found his Young Pirates Edition of World Travel.

"We must be there then!" smiled Mr Bogey.

"Why's that th... " Just before Hairy Mole could finish his sentence a loud screech was heard from the crow's nest.

"Ship ahoy, ship ahoooooooy!"

screamed Guff at the top of her voice.

All the pirates ran to the side of the ship. The little ship started to tip slightly with the weight. But there was nothing to see except sea.

"Noooooo! Ship ahoy, other side, other side!!"

yelled a frustrated Guff.

Sure enough, a beautiful ship with 7 sails, 7 tall and impressive masts and 7 dark and scary cannons came in to view.

Flags of all colours billoWed out into the warm Mediterranean air and the sails blew the ship towards Hairy Mole and his crew.

38

On top of the highest mast was the Italian flag.

Hairy Mole stood next to Mr Bogey, who stood next to Pickle, who was at the side of Crevice and Pit, as they took their place to the right of Belch, who was shoulder to nose with Guff.

"Do not be alarmed men, these Italians are the friendliest sailors on the sea. They will probably invite us on board their beautiful ship for vino and formaggio!" laughed the Hairy Captain.

On board the magnificent vessel the rival Italian pirate crew eyed Hairy Mole's little ship with a distaste usually reserved for something found on the sole of a shoe.

The Italian pirate captain stood with his hands on his hips. The purple plumage of feathers hung from his hat and f
l
o
w
e
d
down his back as though a peacock had landed upon his head.

The Italian captain, whose name was Garibaldi, like the biscuit but with fewer currants, sat back on his golden throne and was instantly fanned by

two golden monkeys.

"Signor Bourbon?" called Captain Garibaldi. He was joined by his first mate, Signor Bourbon. Signor Bourbon also wore a hat with a gigantic green feather, not quite as flamboyant as Captain Garibaldi's but pretty large and colourful all the same.

"Signor Bourbon, what iz thiz little ship I Zee before me?"

Garibaldi pointed a golden-ringed finger in the general direction of Hairy Mole's little ship.

Signor Bourbon looked a little closer. He had to squint his eyes to get a better look.

"It looks like a little non-Italiano ship. Shall we attack them and steal their treasureZ?" asked first mate Bourbon.

"An excellent idea, Signor Bourbon. They will be no match for our 7 cannons and our strong Italiano pirate crew!"

With this, Captain Garibaldi turned around and smiled at the fifty strong Italian pirates before him. Feathers and gold glinted in the sunlight, as the pirates growled in readiness for attack.

"Men, are you ready for an attack on a non-Italiano ship that looks more like a bath than a boat?" The Italian crew growled even louder to express their willingness for battle.

"Si, si!" some of them shouted, which means "Yes, yes!" in Italian.

"Wait for my command! We will be covered in jewels before the day is done."

"Si, si!" shouted the men.

Captain Garibaldi returned to the front of the mighty vessel and stared at the little bath - I mean boat - before him.

"Do they look like **savages** to you, Bourbon?"

Signor Bourbon had been gazing through his telescope while Captain Garibaldi had been making his speech.

"Zey look more like **sausages** to me Captain. Zee for yourself."

Bourbon handed the telescope to his captain, who placed the lens to his right eye and stared.

In the circle of the lens were **7** of the worst-dressed pirates Captain Gar**i**bald**i** had ever seen. As he looked closer he could see that, rather than looking fearless and menacing, the men on the little ship appeared to be smiling and waving!

"Mamma mia!" declared Captain Gar**i**bald**i**.

"Oh yes, they can see us. Keep on waving lads. We will be invited on board for Italian hospitality any second now."

Hairy Mole waved his big warty hand high in the air, as he gave his best cheesy smile to the two Italian pirates who seemed to be wearing exotic birds on their heads.

"Any minute now," smiled Hairy Mole through gritted, cheesy (in every sense of the word) teeth.

Just as it looked like their smiles would pop their cheeks, the pirates saw a small rowing boat being lowered from the side of the Italian ship.

On board the rowing boat were three men. One of the men was wearing a peacock, one of the men was wearing a parrot and the third man looked very gruff but still managed to be covered in jewels and also had a bird on his head, possibly a pigeon. The gruff pirate with the pigeon rowed the peacock and parrot Pirates alongside Hairy Mole's ship.

45

As they came closer it was clear that the Italian pirates were not interested in any kind of invitation of Italian hospitality.

Captain Garibaldi got straight to the point: "Ahoy! You bunch of tatty-clothed, non-Italiano, smelly-looking pirates."

"Ahoy!" called Hairy Mole and his crew, as this was the only word that they actually understood.

Garibaldi continued carefully, standing on the edge of the rowing boat, hands on hips and chest out for full effect.

"We were going to attack you and steal whatever treasures you may aV!" Garibaldi shouted. "It iZ now obvious to myself and Signor Bourbon that you aV NOTHINK! Apart from bad hair and probably very, very smelly bottomZ!"

"What is he saying Hairy Mole?" whispered Mr Bogey.

"I think he is welcoming us to his country and asking if we would like some jam," answered Hairy Mole, his eyes now fixed on Garibaldi's amazing feathered hat.

"Leave this to me, Hairy Mole," said Mr Bogey.

"Si, si!" squeaked Mr Bogey down to the shiny Italian Captain.

They all smiled as the three men on the rowing boat held their bellies with laughter.

"I told you they were a friendly bunch!" beamed Hairy Mole. "Well done, Bogey!" he added.

"You even admit it, you smelly-bottomed, tatty pirates!" shouted up Captain Garibaldi.

"As we are obviously far superior and far better dressed than any of you will ever be, in the history of the world that aZ not yet happened, we will insult you by giving you a box full of our oldest, smelliest clothes, including our pants, as a mark of our lack of respect to all you non-Italiano pirates."

The pirate with the pigeon on his head hauled a box onto his shoulders and proceeded to climb up the side of the ship.

"Quick lads, help him on board."

As the surly yet impeccably dressed pirate clambered on to the deck, the crew gathered round until they all stood in silence, staring at each other.

"You make me want to cry with your smelliness and bad hair! Your Mamas must be monkeys and your Papas must be the frogs!" With that, the Italian pirate with the pigeon on his head placed the box down onto the deck and climbed back down to the rowing boat below.

"Even our pants!" he called up, before joining his Captain.

"What did he say, Hairy Mole? What did he say?" The crew crowded around their Captain, as the rowing boat containing the three Italian pirates rowed away.

"I think they said that they were too busy to see us at the moment, but we should accept this as a gift from their Mamas and Papas!"

Hairy Mole undid the box and revealed the colourful silks and shiny pants inside.

"OOOOOOO O O OOOOOO!"

gasped

the crew

as they gawped at the various garments.

"Grazi, grazi! Ciao, ciao!" called out Hairy Mole to the disappearing rowing boat.

"I pity you and I pity my old pants, smelly bottomz!" shouted out Captain Garibaldi, as he waved a jewel-covered hand.

The crew waved back: Hairy Mole wearing a 'new' hat with a golden feather, Mr Bogey wearing a 'new' waistcoat with shiny buttons, Crevice and Pit marvelling at their find of golden buckled boots, and Pickle, Belch and Guff wearing the finest purple silk pants over the tops of their trousers.

The Italian pirate ship began to sail out of sight as Hairy Mole and his crew shook each other by the hands and admired each other's garments.

"If this is a slice of Italy, then bring me the whole pie!" squeaked Mr Bogey. Everyone heartily agreed and they smiled and laughed until finally it was time for bed.

Chapter Five

Hungry Pirates

The next morning Hairy Mole was to be found sitting cross-legged at the front of the little ship. As he stared at the spiralling

birds in the sky and tweaked the golden feather on his 'new' hat, his mind drifted to his hero Blackbeard the Pirate. Hairy remembered the poster on his bedroom wall with Blackbeard standing with a large toothless grin on his warty face and an equally large, black boot squashing the chest of some decapitated villager, who had obviously been a victim to Blackbeard's villainy and bad pirate ways.

Hairy Mole continued to think of what Blackbeard would do in his situation. As he thought, he plucked at a long curly hair that had started to grow from the tip of his bulging nose.

Poink! went the hair, as it was released from the greasy skin that had been ever such a good breeding ground for spots, pimples and hairs. Rather, in fact, like the hair that Hairy Mole now twiZZled in between two fingers as he thought of what to do.

"Aaaaa tissshooooo!!!!" sneezed Mr Bogey as he sat down beside Hairy Mole.

"This 'new' waistcoat has given me a cold, Hairy Mole!" snuffled Mr Bogey.

"Well, if you will wear it without any undershirt I'm not surprised," said Hairy Mole, shaking his head at the half-naked Bogey.

"I need medicine!" sniffed the First Mate.

"Well, I need food!" Hairy Mole shouted.

Without further ado, he jumped to his feet and called his men to order.

Belch, Pickle, Crevice and Pit, Guff and Mr Bogey stood in line, all wearing their Italian silks and boots.

Hairy Mole began to pace back and forth, back and forth, in front of the smelly, but shiny, pirates. He squinted his eyes and rubbed his chin whilst looking over his shabby crew.

"Now!" Hairy Mole started, and then remembered the look that Blackbeard had on his face in the poster above his bed.

"**Now!**" he began again, this time grimacing and growling just like **Blackbeard.**

"I am hungry and I am a pirate. Grrrrrrrr!" growled Hairy Mole for extra-fierce effect.

"Do you know what that makes me?" he continued to growl.

"Grrrrrrrrrrrrrr!"

Guff raised her hand.

"Grruuff?" Hairy Mole growled.

"Guff!" Guff corrected.

"What?" asked a confused Hairy Mole.

"My name is Guff, that's all. You said Grruuff and my name is Guff!" Guff pointed out to her growling pirate captain.

"I know your name is Guff. Now, what do I become if I am hungry and a pirate?" Hairy Mole was pretty close to losing his patience, as Guff had stood on his last nerve by practically ruining his pirate speech.

"A hungry pirate?" Guff whispered quietly.

"Whaaaat?" Hairy Mole raged.

"Well, if you are a pirate, which you are, and if you are hungry, which you normally are, that makes you a hungry pirate!" Guff proudly arrived at her answer.

There were general nods of agreement and congratulations for the young pirate. So much so, the other pirates lifted her above their heads and started to sing: "For she's a jolly good Guff, for she's a jolly good Guff, for she's a jolly good Guuuuuufff, she got an answer right!"

Their song was rudely interrupted before they could launch into the next chorus.

"No, no, no, no, NO!" By now Hairy Mole's last nerve had not only been stood on, but it had been pulled, torn, ripped and tickled.

"No!" he added for good measure.

"A pirate that is hungry can only mean one thing!" Hairy Mole shouted, until his ears smoked and a tiny spot on his neck burst, releasing some green goo onto the back of his collar.

"DANGEROUS!" he bellowed, looking at his crew.

"We are dangerous, bad pirates with fire in our hearts and a growl in our bellies."

"Aaaaa tissshooooo!!!!"

sneezed Mr Bogey.

"Buuuurp!"

belched Belch.

"Almost, Belch, almost." Hairy Mole wiped his brow.

"I *am* pretty hungry, now you come to mention it," said Belch, rubbing his big belly.

"I haven't brushed my teeth for three weeks!" declared Pickle. "That's pretty dangerous!" Everyone heartily agreed and moved a little further away from smelly breath Pickle.

"How about the kind of dangerous where we attack that village, taking their food and squashing their flowers?"

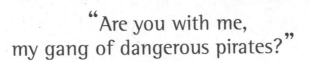

With that Hairy Mole began to pull on a thin rope that was attached to the top of the mast. When the rope reached the top, a black flag unravelled to reveal a skull and crossed bones.

"Are you with me,
my gang of dangerous pirates?"

Hairy Mole looked at his crew, who currently looked neither dangerous, nor with anything.

"Aaaaatissshoooooo!" squeaked Mr Bogey in a display of cold and solidarity.

"We're with you, Hairy Mole!" called out Crevice and Pit, who weren't really interested in danger. They were just fed up with fish fingers.

Pickle, Guff and Belch all agreed that it was high time for a bit of danger, and they pulled up their purple pants and began to sharpen their cutlasses, in a show of just how rough and tough they intended to be.

All the time the crew were preparing themselves, land - and the little Italian village - was getting ever closer.

Chapter Six

Attack!

Now, it just so happened that the little Italian village that Hairy Mole and his 'dangerous' pirate crew were thinking of attacking was doing a bit of preparing itself. Large wooden tables had been set out and were being covered with various meats, breads and fruits. Huge bottles of vino were lining the entire table and all the Italian villagers were busy laughing and singing while they d a n c e d around the feast. As Hairy Mole's little ship pulled ashore, the villagers looked up and sang with glee.

"Guests! LOOk everybody, we have de guests."

Now, as everybody knows, there is nothing more that an Italian loves than a guest for tea. It gives them an opportunity to celebrate how good they are at cooking and how thoroughly hospitable they are to everybody, including pirates.

Hairy Mole and his crew stood aboard the little ship as it calmly floated on the shallow waters of the bay. Each man was armed, or rather teethed, with a cutlass and together they growled like a pack of wild animals (possibly beavers!).

"Almost dare min!" Hairy Mole mumbled through his gritted, cutlass-bearing teeth.

"Wod?" Mr Bogey squeaked back through his equally full mouth.

"I dared, we're almost dare!" replied Hairy Mole.

"Doh, I dee!" nodded Mr Bogey.

The shore became closer and the men prepared to jump on to the sand and attack the unsuspecting villagers.

"Dow, on di count of dee," gritted Hairy Mole.

"Wod?"

This time all of the crew turned to their leader to find out exactly what he was dalking, I mean talking, about.

Removing the cutlass from his mouth, being careful not to cut himself, Hairy Mole spoke again.

"I said, on the count of thr ... "

"Cor can do dell dat?" announced Belch, rubbing his belly and lifting his nose high into the air.

"Take the cutlass out, Belch my boy!" Hairy Mole advised.

"Dorry, I mean sorry!" said Belch, removing the cutlass not so carefully and just tweaking the corner of his mouth.

"Ouch! I said, can you smell that? Go on, lift your hairy nostrils to the air and get them itching."

With that, everybody flared their nostrils and sniffed at the air.

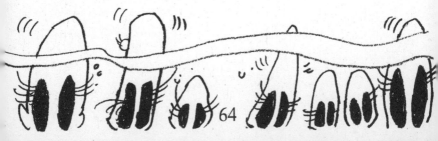

A smell of tender, succulent roasting meat filled their senses. Fresh herbs and spices travelled up their passages and into their brains; the brains told the bellies and the bellies rumbled with approval.

Hairy Mole and his crew were so overcome by the magnificent smells that filled their minds that they quite simply forgot what they were doing. In a trance they floated from the little ship and onto the beach.

The villagers welcomed them and sat them down at the l o n g table. Hairy Mole took pride of place at the head of the table and smiled with delight as he was presented with dish upon dish of gorgeous food.

dish
dish
dish   dish
dish
dish

Mr Bogey, who was unable to smell the food due to a rather nasty cold, nudged Hairy Mole in the ribs.

"Eh, Mr Bogey, what is occurring?" Hairy Mole gazed back at Mr Bogey with an extremely contented grin on his face.

"When do we attack, boss? I mean dis is all well and good, dut to be honest I dan't actually smell a dean, danks to dis rotten dold!" sniffed Bogey.

"Take your cutlass out of your mouth when you're eating, Bogey!" Hairy Mole sighed.

"It is out of my mouth!" snorted Mr Bogey. "The men want to know when to attack. Look at dem. They are getting very restless!" Mr Bogey cast an arm over at the men to indicate their restlessness.

Pickle, Guff, the twins and Belch all looked about as restless as a cat that had just got the cream and then found the keys to the dairy! Their faces were awash with happiness as they communicated their pleasure with grunts, smiles and nods. The Italian villagers were most pleased and patted the men on the shoulders, and the old ladies squeezed their cheeks as if testing the ripeness of peaches.

"Yes, yes, Mr Bogey, I see what you mean. Urrm, give it another few minutes, eh?" Hairy Mole tucked into another plate of pasta that an overjoyed Italian villager had placed in front of him.

"Ziz food makes you into big strong men!" laughed the villager, happy with his guest's obvious enjoyment.

"Si, si!" replied Hairy Mole through a mouthful of spaghetti.

"What did he day, Hairy Mole?" snuffled Mr Bogey.

"I think he said that there was plenty more where that came from. Now tuck in, Bogey."

Mr Bogey folded his arms and watched the men laughing and joking and having a marvellous time. Poor Bogey couldn't taste a thing due to his cold, so he sat and waited for Hairy Mole to give the order to attack.

It wasn't long before buckles were unbuckled and buttons began to pop.

The crew had thoroughly enjoyed themselves and their hosts' wonderful generosity. So much so that they had completely forgotten the reason that they were there in the first place.

As the sun started to set and the villagers cleaned away the plates and empty bowls, everyone sat back in their chairs and sighed with full, contented bellies.

Everyone except Mr Bogey. Suddenly he leapt to his feet, cutlass in hand.

"ATTACK!" he cried. "Come on men, come on Hairy Mole. Attack!!!"

"Oh yeah, I forgot about the attacking," said Pickle, wiping his mouth with the back of his sleeve.

"Do we have to?" asked Guff sleepily.

Hairy Mole sat at the head of the table and looked at Mr Bogey waving his cutlass around.

"Mr Bogey, sit down, why don't you? We have been shown the finest hospitality by the friendliest people. There will be no attacking today. In fact, quite the opposite." Hairy Mole stood up with his cutlass in the air.

"Thank you, villagers, for such a marvellous feast. I shall leave my cutlass with you as a gift and a token of our friendship.

You can use it for cutting the meat or perhaps as a decorative ornament above your fireplace, it is up to you."

Hairy Mole presented his cutlass to the chief villager.

Mr Bogey looked quite embarrassed as he quickly stood next to Hairy Mole.

"I too leave my cutlass as a gesture of good will. I have had a very bad cold recently and couldn't actually taste a thing. However, it did look very nice. Well done!" squeaked Mr Bogey, a dribble of goo hanging from the end of his nose.

He handed his cutlass to a villager and sheepishly followed the rest of the crew as

70

they waddled their way back to the ship, being slapped on the back and shaking hands with the villagers as they left.

As the crew boarded the boat, the head Italian villager turned to his friend.

"What did ee zay?"

"I think the s q u e a k y one thought the pasta brought tears to his eyes and the hairy one thought the pollo was as dolce as the setting sun!"

With that, they both nodded happily and waved enthusiastically until the pirates had sailed out of sight.

Chapter Seven

Water, Water, Everywhere

Hairy Mole and his six, by now, fat and contented pirates sat on the deck of the little ship as it bobbed up and down, up and down, on the calm waters of the Mediterranean. None of the pirates spoke as they stretched and lazed in the sun.

Pickle dipped his eXtra-large toes into the water, as the shimmer from the sea danced across the waves created by the gentle movement of the ship as it drifted on the water.

Crevice and Pit were splishing and splashing their extra-large fingers behind the little ship, catching the bubbles as they floated off the water.

Belch sniffed in the salty air that made him even sleepier, as he curled his large bottom into a coil of thick oily rope.

Guff was resting in the crow's nest, listening to the far-off cries of the gulls and the gurgling, rushing sound of water slowly working its way through a hole in the bottom of the ship.

Mr Bogey was idly dripping linseed oil onto his leg, 1 mean bat, as he polished and shined his precious appendage.

73

In a hammock Hairy Mole rocked and swayed and dreamed of high adventure and carrots.

The carrots d a n c e d around his head, as the effect of far too much cheese for his tea started to turn the carrots to birds, and the birds to leaves, and the leaves into beautiful coloured butterflies that flitted and floated from mountain to wave, from wave to mountain, from mountain to wa ...

But wait a minute!!! Enough cheesy dream time, what about ... ????

"WATER! There's water!"

Guff screamed at the top of her voice, shattering the calm and making Hairy Mole's butterflies disappear into a cloud of fuzzy-eyed smoke.

"Yes, yes Guff, it's called the sea, you clodhopper! I'm surprised you haven't noticed it before!" Hairy Mole raised an eyebrow up to the crow's nest where little Guff was a shriekin' and a hollerin'.

"No, no, down below, water down below!"

Guff yelled again as she shimmied her way down the rigging.

"Water down below? Well there's no need to make a jig and a shake about it," said Hairy Mole, raising a bushy eyebrow at Guff as she clambered down the rigging and onto the deck.

"I don't know why she can't go over the side like everybody else," mumbled Belch, as he shifted his bottom in the coil of rope.

"No, you nincompoops, we're sinking!" yelled Guff, as she jumped on to the deck.

Now, down in the hold a very small knOthOle from a particularly not very special plank of wood had managed to lo^{O}sen itself. Now, unfortunately, this not very special plank of wood was at the $_{bottom}$ of the little ship, so now it had become quite special indeed, as the water began to seep into the hold below.

Hairy Mole appeared from down below with a ghostly look on his face. The little knothole letting in the water had now become a gaping, gaWping hole and the little trickle of water had become a spurting, spewing fountain.

"All hands to the pump! Crevice and Pit, get your extra-large hands to work and start bailing!" Hairy Mole's wide eyes told a story of fear. In his head he wondered whether this was the end, was this the way his adventures would finish, before they had even begun? Not if he could help it!

The crew lined up with buckets and they passed them back and forth from the hold to the side of the ship. The water sloshed and splashed over the side as the buckets and the crew worked at a terrific speed. No one had time to think as they passed the buckets that were filled by Crevice and Pit.

The water was, by now, increasing at a horrific rate, and the nails in the wooden floor were pinging and popping as the sea quickly found its way into the hold.

Crevice and Pit emerged like two wet puppies. Their hands were swollen from the constant surge of water against their buckets and their wild, frightened eyes shimmered as they made their way out of the dark hold and into the bright sunshine.

The crew dropped their buckets and looked to Hairy Mole.

"What are we going to do, Hairy Mole?" squeaked Mr Bogey in an even higher voice than usual. Hairy Mole looked at his beaten crew as they stood wet and shivering. The little ship was slowly sinking. Overhead the sun beat down and the seagulls circled, squawking and crying above, as they watched the brave little ship battle against the sea.

"Men, we are sinking!" Hairy Mole began, rather obviously. "We need to head for land as soon as possible. Then we may have to swim for it." As he spoke, Hairy Mole searched the horizon for a hint of mountain or a suggestion of land.

"There, Hairy Mole, there everyone, land ahoy!"

Guff yelled at the top of her voice.

Sure enough, in the very far distance, to the East, a small dark lump could be seen against the skyline.

"We'll never make it!" squeaked Mr Bogey.

"It's true, Hairy Mole," continued Crevice and Pit, "we're taking in more water than we are bailing out. We have half an hour maximum before this ship becomes a submarine and we become fish food!" Mr Bogey was wringing his hands and pacing backwards and forwards.

"We need help, men, and we need it fast!" The crew looked at each other for answers, then they looked to the sky.

Something was happening overhead. The sky had turned from blue to white and the sun had become covered by feathered wings, creating a dark shadow across the sea and the little ship.

"The seagulls! It's our friends the seagulls!" Guff raised her hands above her head as the fluttering and flapping became louder. The noise from the wings was eventually so loud that Guff had to cover her extra-large ears for fear of becoming deafened.

A particularly familiar-looking bird perched right on top of Belch's head.

"Hello, Hairy Mole," said Toby the Seagull.

Toby's calmness reassured the crew, his wise eyes twinkling as he winked with a comforting smile.

Chapter Eight

Up, Up and Away

Hairy Mole and his crew watched in amazement as Toby squawked instructions to the thousands of circling seagulls. One by one they landed on the ship: some grabbed the sides, some gripped the sails and others clung on to the ropes. There the seagulls watched, each clasping every piece of space available, as they waited for Toby.

"Are you ready to fly, Hairy Mole?" Toby asked with a smile.

"I would rather fly than swim, Mr Seagull!" replied Hairy Mole, safe in the knowledge that help was at hand.

With that Toby flew to the top of the mast and with one seagull word from his seagull beak, the other birds raised their wings above their backs and slowly lowered them to their sides. Again they repeated the process. Up and down went the thousand seagull wings, as if one giant bird was preparing to fly. The crew fell to the floor in wonder and amazement as the movement of the wings blew a warm breeze over their bodies, and slowly they began to move.

The little ship was very heavy due to the weight of the water trapped in the hold, and each seagull stretched and strained in the bright sunlight. As the birds began to spread their wings, so the little ship was lifted further and further out of the sea. The hole in the bottom of the ship began to drain and it wasn't long before the flying became easier as the water poured from the ship and back to the sea below.

"Hairy Mole, this is amazing!" laughed Pickle, as he stretched out his extra-large feet and let them dry in the warm breeze, as the seagulls flapped their beautiful wings.

Everyone stared at the sky above as the clouds and the sun became even closer.

The ship soared into the air, leaving the remaining droplets of water to fall back down, down, down to the sea.

Down below, another vessel with spectacular sails and a fifty-strong pirate crew sailed on the sea. The fifty strong pirates gasped in awe at the miracle above them.

"I don't believe it, the smelly piratZ aV a flying ship. Their bottomZ must be blowing out so much hot gaZ that they are taking off into space!"

Captain Garibaldi looked skywards, and just as he did so a large seagull poo landed right on his shiny, feathered hat.

85

Signor Bourbon held out his hand: "Hhmmmm! Lookz like it iz starting to rain!" he mentioned, just before receiving a whack on the back of his head from Captain Garibaldi's freshly coated hat.

Hairy Mole's little ship flew high into the air, over islands and shimmering waves, over fish and the spurting whales, one of which looked very familiar. Clouds passed underneath as the ship sailed through the sky as if it were on a tranquil lake of blue and white.

"Homeward bound, Hairy Mole?" asked Toby, settling on Belch's head.

"Homeward bound, Toby," smiled Hairy Mole, and he settled back into his hammock and let the gentle flapping of wings send him to sleep.

Chapter Nine

A Heroes' Welcome

When Hairy Mole awoke, the ship was slowly being lowered onto dry land. All the locals had come out to welcome them home, and Mr Barnacle rubbed his hands together with glee as he spied the gaping hole in the ship's bottom.

The little ship was gently tipped onto her side as she came to rest on the concrete jetty surrounding the harbour. The seagulls squawked and cawed in delight, as they too had been part of a fantastic adventure.

Postmaster Will, Mrs Gumdrop and Mr Lockley the Innkeeper stood with the other villagers and cheered and applauded as Hairy Mole and his pirate crew let down the gangplank and strode onto the concrete jetty, like heroes.

Mrs Bulbous Mole made her way through the crowd to greet her son and his crew. They all hugged and kissed and praised Toby, whilst backslapping each other.

"My boy, my boy, my smelly, hairy boy!" cried Mrs Mole. "You are indeed a great pirate to return to us with so many stories, hats, full bellies and silky pants. All I ask of you now is one thing!" smiled Mrs Bulbous Mole.

There was a hush over the crowd.

"SSSSSSSSSSSSSSSSHHHHHHHHHHHHHuuuuuuuuuHHHHHHHHHHhhhhhhhh!!!" shushed the crowd.

"Anything mother. What do you ask?" Hairy Mole looked at his mother and took off his 'new' hat.

"Just keep my kitchen tidy after you have done your cooking."

With this, Toby flew on to Bulbous Mole's shoulder.

"Fish pie would be delightful, Hairy Mole! Just remember: Barry, Larry and Peter don't like cod, and Helen, Susan and Valerie aren't very fond of pepper!"

With that, a large squawking and cheering took place as all the seagulls flew high into the air and landed on the roof of the Moles' cottage.

Hairy Mole stepped forward.

"Thank you everyone: my friends on the land, my friends on the sea and my friends in the sky. One final thing, as I'm not accustomed to making speeches: last one in the kitchen does the washing up!"

With that, Hairy Mole and his pirate crew ran to the cottage to make a thousand fish pies: three without cod and three without pepper.